The Newbie's Guide to Positive Parenting

Second Edition

Copyright Rebecca Eanes 2015
All rights reserved.

ISBN-13: 978-1507580011

ISBN-10: 1507580010

About the Author

Rebecca Eanes is an international bestselling author, founder of Positive-parents.org, and creator of the Facebook community Positive Parenting: Toddlers and Beyond. Rebecca has also co-authored the book, Positive Parenting in Action: The How-To Guide to Putting Positive Parenting Principles into Action in Early Childhood, with Laura Ling. She is the grateful mother to two boys.

All opinions expressed in this book are her own and derive from years of research and parenting.

Information contained in this book should not be construed as professional or medical advice.

Author photo credit, back cover: Carolina Weatherford

Disclaimer

This book is designed to provide information on positive parenting only. This information is provided and sold with the knowledge that the publisher and author do not offer any legal or professional advice. In the case of a need for any such expertise, consult with the appropriate professional. This book does not contain all information available on the subject. This book has not been created to be specific to any individual's or organizations' situation or needs. Every effort has been made to make this book as accurate as possible. However, there may be typographical and/or content errors. Therefore, this book should serve only as a general guide and not as the ultimate source of subject information. This book contains information that might be dated and is intended only to educate and entertain. The author and publisher shall have no liability or responsibility to any person or entity regarding any loss or damage incurred, or alleged to have incurred, directly or indirectly, by the information contained in this book. You hereby agree to be bound by this disclaimer or you may return this book within the guarantee time period for a full refund.

For my sons who are the smile in my heart and the light of my world. Thank you for inspiring me, loving me, and healing me. You are amazing people, and I am honored to be your mommy. I love you both to the moon and back.

Table of Contents

Introduction

Allow me to begin my writings to you by telling you a short tale. This particular tale is my own, but I suspect that it may feel quite familiar to the eyes reading this page. It is a tale of excitement, love, heartache, trials, and adventure. I can't tell you how the story ends because, well, I'm still in the middle of the book. I'm making it up as I go along - filling in a fresh blank page every day. Then, I turn the page and wait to see what tomorrow brings. These pages will one day be my legacy. This is how it began...

It was the day after Christmas in the year 2006. Standing in my little bathroom, in a home tucked away by the mountainside, I stood with my hands shaking. My heart was pounding out of my chest. The tile floor was ice cold beneath my bare feet, my reflection showed hope and anticipation in tired-looking eyes, and never had two minutes lasted longer. My mind was swirling with a dozen thoughts as I watched the hourglass turn over and over and over again. It stopped.

PREGNANT.

I picked up the test with my shaky hands just to make

sure I had read it right. I had seen so many *not pregnants* before that I thought perhaps I just wasn't seeing the *not* in that particular light. I held it up right in front of my eyes. They had not deceived me. It did, indeed, say *pregnant.*

Nine months (or so) later, I gave birth to the most perfect and beautiful child ever in the history of ever. (What, you too?) A baby boy. A baby boy whose very existence changed the entire world for me in one breath, one cry, one single moment. Oh, how I loved this boy with a fierce and wild love like I'd never felt before in my life. I wanted to hold him in my arms forever and ever, and I never wanted that moment to end.

But all moments end. And new moments begin.

I scribbled magnificent stories of first roll-overs, milestones, baby food mishaps, and peek-a-boo as the pages of time turned ever so quickly. First smiles, crawling, first words, standing, first steps, songs, giggles, and delightful squeals told the captivating tale of the happiest mother in the world and the smallest love of her life.

Eighteen months later, I stood once more on a cold tile

floor with shaking hands, though in a different house tucked away by a different mountain. My heart doubled in size that day. My tummy quadrupled in size over the next several months, and once again, I gave birth to the most perfect and beautiful child ever in the history of ever. A baby boy. A baby boy whose very existence changed the entire world for me in one breath, one cry, one single moment. Oh, how I loved this little boy with a fierce, wild, but familiar love. I wanted to hold him in my arms forever and ever, and I never wanted that moment to end.

But as I said...

I quickly scrawled more exquisite stories on my blank pages - a story of brothers meeting for the first time, two souls orchestrated by God to share childhoods together, and it was breathtaking to watch the story unfold. A story of a mother falling head over heels for a second smiling, giggling, rolling little love whose dark brown eyes made her melt into a puddle of ridiculous adoration was written in those pages.

Then, the stories began to change. My love stories were sprinkled with stories of frustration and desperation, and little by little, those stories became more and more until one sad day, when I looked back through the book, most of the pages I saw were marked up with disappointment and regret.

What happened to my wonderful story? This story was filled with tears and time-outs. This story was filled with disappointment and disconnection. I didn't like it. This was not my story. I refused to continue to fill the pages of our lives with weeping and woe.

Brokenhearted and desperately wanting back the bond I once shared with my little loves, I set out on a journey to reclaim what was lost. And that is how I discovered positive parenting.

1

What is Positive Parenting?

Positive parenting isn't a method, a set of rules, or a style. Positive parenting is a philosophy, a way of relating to children and to ourselves. Positive parenting – sometimes referred to as positive discipline, gentle guidance, or love-based parenting – is guidance offered in a positive way, keeping in mind the dignity of the parent and child and preserving the parent-child relationship.

Positive parenting is about believing in the altruism of our children, believing that they want to do what is good. It is about believing that behavior is a form of communication and clues us in to what is going on inside the child. Positive parenting is also about being firm and kind, consistent and empathetic, and viewing disagreements between parents and children as opportunities to develop problem-solving skills and learn how to navigate relationships.

There are 5 principles from which positive parenting actions derive:

1. Attachment. According to English psychiatrist, John Bowlby, and American psychologist, Mary Ainsworth, who pioneered the *attachment theory*, the mother-child bond is the primary force in infant development. Scientific evidence has proven that children are hardwired to connect, and if that connection isn't there, then the brain may not develop properly.

The attachment bond theory states that the bond between infants and primary caregivers is responsible for:

• shaping all of our future relationships
• strengthening or damaging our abilities to focus, be conscious of our feelings, and calm ourselves
• the ability to bounce back from misfortune"[1]

When a *secure* attachment is made, the child feels safe and understood. *Insecure* attachment occurs when the infant does not have consistent, nurturing care. Having a trusted caregiver who consistently provides care, affection, and support to the child in infancy and early childhood is important for a child to reach his or her full potential.

2. Respect. Respect isn't a privilege, it's an emotional

need. Children need to be treated in a thoughtful, attentive, civil, and courteous manner. As individuals and as human beings, they deserve the same consideration as others. The best way children learn about respect is to feel what it's like to be treated respectfully by those around them.

3. Proactive parenting. Proactive parents respond instead of react. Responding quite simply means there is a planned action, a forethought into how you will respond to your child and to certain behaviors. Reactive parents act impulsively. Being proactive also means addressing a potential problem behavior at the first sign, before it snowballs into a real problem.

4. Empathetic leadership. Empathy is the oil that keeps relationships running smoothly. Not to be confused with permissive parents, positive parents are still in a leadership role. Being empathetic means we understand the needs of our children, and that helps us to develop a closer relationship with them.

5. Positive discipline. Punishment is distinct from discipline. The goal of punishment is to make someone suffer enough to cause them to want to avoid that particular behavior (and therefore punishment) again in the future. The goal of discipline is to teach someone

to control impulses and behavior, to learn new skills, and to fix mistakes and find solutions. Positive discipline isn't about making a child pay for his mistake but rather learn from it.

Why Choose Positive Parenting?

There are many benefits of positive parenting. Most important is the secure attachment between parent and child, which encourages healthy development. Secure attachment builds resilience[2], paves the way for how well your child will function as an adult in a relationship, and has a positive impact on brain development.

Positive parenting encourages children to develop self-discipline and offers more benefits compared to punishments, time-outs, and scolding. Some of these benefits include:

1. A stronger parent-child relationship in which the child wants to behave because of the strong bond formed with the parent. This involves setting the child up for success and recognizing good behaviors. While punishments can damage the relationship and make the child focus on getting even or on his anger with the

parent rather than on the behavior, loving guidance allows the relationship to remain intact so the child can focus on improving behavior.

2. Emotional intelligence, or EQ, is recognizing, validating, and teaching children about their emotions and how to navigate them. Clinical psychologist, Dr. Laura Markham of Ahaparenting.com says that the core components of a high EQ[3] are emotional self-knowledge and self-acceptance, sensitivity to the cues of others, empathy (which can be defined as the ability to see and feel something from the other's point of view), and the ability to regulate one's own anxiety in order to talk about emotionally charged issues in a constructive way.

3. Reduction in power struggles and misbehavior. Limits set and enforced with empathy help the child to better accept these limits. As our children feel more connected to us, cooperation naturally follows.

Understanding basic brain development is a big factor in why I chose positive parenting. This is a very simplistic model of a very complex organ, but think of the brain in terms of two parts – an upper brain and a lower brain. The lower brain is fully developed at birth and regulates functions like breathing, digestion, reflexes, and heart rate. The upper brain is developing in infancy and continues to develop throughout childhood, not reaching maturation until the mid 20's! The upstairs brain is responsible for emotions control, empathy, and complex thinking.

 This information is key to understanding behaviors such as tantrums and aggression, because when you realize that a toddler simply does not have the cognitive capability to pause and reflect (a function of the underdeveloped upstairs brain), suddenly you understand that this isn't poor behavior but purely an issue of brain development. This knowledge helps us provide empathy and understanding in situations which would otherwise cause us a lot of frustration.

Right about now, you may have one eyebrow raised in skepticism. Believe me, I understand. I, too, was quite skeptical when I first began exploring this philosophy. To me, it sounded positively marvelous but not at all practical – much like riding my unicorn through a field of rainbow tulips.

I wish I could tell you that my journey from fear-based to love-based parenting was an easy straight shot, but that wouldn't be the truth. The truth is that my road to positive parenting was more of a long, winding road

Your Library Name: SOUTH HUNTINGTON LIBRARY

Your Name: KAREN

Your E-mail:

To: SCLS Original Cataloging

MAT'L TYPE	TITLE	ISBN, ISSN, OTHER NO.	TOTAL ITEMS
BOOK	THE NEWBIE'S GUIDE TO POSITIVE PARENTING	9781507580011	1

1. Enter your Library Name, your name and email address
2. Stamp or mark your item with your Library Name and Address
3. Send two copies of this form with the item

Record Created:

B 48225137

Date Sent To SCLS	Date Received AT SCLS	Cataloged By	SKY # Added	Date Returned To Library
KD 3/18/15	3/23	Tm	274374383	4 – 6

with lots of zigzags, roadblocks, and crazy loops on which I got lost more than a few times. It takes no small leap of faith to push aside everything you've been told about raising children and about what it means to be a child.

I suppose, like many of you, I had the hardest time understanding what I was supposed to do in lieu of punishment. What was the point of having rules if there were no punishments for breaking them? What was I supposed to do when my child misbehaved or stepped out of the boundaries I had established? (I will help you solve this mystery in the later chapters of this book.)

I wanted easy answers to these questions. I wanted step-by-step instructions on what to do when my child did X, Y, and Z, but you see, I was missing the point of positive parenting entirely. Positive parenting isn't about telling you what you should and shouldn't do but rather about helping you and me tune out the clamor of the world and tune in to the whispers of our hearts. Everything you need to know about loving, correcting, and guiding your child is already within you, but it often gets buried underneath all the rubble of *shoulds* and *should nots* that culture has infiltrated our minds with.

Therefore, the ideas for problem-solving and alternatives to punishment I offer to you within these pages are simply to help you understand what it may look like to implement this philosophy in your home. These are the tools that I have used in my own family that helped us. However, you are the expert on your child, and your unique relationship will determine how you parent. There is no rule book. Let your heart be your guide.

It took me about a year to wrap my head around this and embrace it wholeheartedly, and I am forever glad that I stayed the course because my own family has been transformed.

I don't want to falsely paint a picture of perfection. This is by no means an easy path to take. It takes a great deal of dedication and work to gently and lovingly tend to the garden of a child's character. It can take time for the seeds you plant to bear fruit, and in that time, when you can't see what's growing just beneath the surface, you may think this isn't working at all. It takes courage to persist when you do not see immediate change, but I encourage you to have courage, dear parent. You will reap what you sow.

2

This is Not Permissive Parenting

Unfortunately, parenting often gets polarized into two types, strict and permissive. There is a misunderstanding when someone suggests that positive parents are permissive parents who fail to set appropriate boundaries, let our children run wild, and fail to discipline them whatsoever. Permissive parenting is not healthy, and I certainly do not advocate being permissive.

I will run through a couple of scenarios to show what positive parenting looks like in contrast to permissive parenting.

Scenario
Your 18 month old is a little explorer. She really likes to climb, too! She can even climb up in the chair, then up onto the kitchen table.

Permissive reaction: "Honey, I told you not to climb. Please get down." No action is taken. "Honey, I asked you to get down. You might fall." At this point, the permissive parent may not take action and hope for the best or finally go remove the child from the table.

Positive reaction: The first time your child attempts to climb on the table, you intervene, saying, "Climbing is fun! Let's find a safe place for you to climb. This table is not safe." Let her climb over some couch cushions, if she wants. Climbing itself is not a misbehavior. She may conquer Mount Everest one day! The goal is to keep her safe and teach her what is appropriate. The next time she heads for the table, immediately and gently take her from the table, repeating the above. If she gets upset, acknowledge her upset. "I see you're mad. You want to climb, but that isn't safe. Let's go play over here."

The positive parent set the limit, stuck to the limit by not allowing the child to climb on the table, but showed the child an appropriate outlet and empathized with her feelings.

Scenario
You have a 5 year old and a 2 year old, and you had to come to the store to pick up a few items. Your 5 year old is begging for a new toy and your 2 year old is late for his nap and is cranky.

Permissive reaction: Buys both kids a new toy *and* a sucker to appease them until the shopping is done.

Positive reaction: To the 5 year old, "That is such a cool toy! I wish I could buy it for you. I can't buy it today, but I will put it on your wish list." If your child continues to ask for the toy, you can say, "You really want that toy! I see how much you want it. It's disappointing when we can't get something we want right away." Empathize with his disappointment. We all get disappointed when we can't get stuff we want. To the 2 year old, "I know you're tired. Will you be my helper? I'm looking for bananas. Do you see any bananas?" It's also not a bad idea to carry things in your purse that you know your child likes, such as a small drawing pad or balloons filled with playdough to toy with.

The positive parent showed leadership by being prepared and skillfully using tools from the positive parenting toolkit - *fantasizing* with the child with "that is a cool toy, I wish I could buy it for you," *empathy* with "I see how much you want it. It's disappointing when we can't get something we want right away" and "I know you're tired," and *redirection* with "will you be my helper? I'm looking for bananas."

Scenario

Your 2 year old has started hitting. At a play date, someone snatches her toy, and she whacks the snatcher with a right hand.

Permissive reaction: Ignores the hitting, blames the other child, or nonchalantly says "we don't hit" from across the room.

Positive reaction: Goes to child immediately and removes her from the situation, gets down on her level and says, "You're mad! She took your toy and you got mad! Hitting hurts. Sit here with me until you're feeling calmer." Have her remain on your lap or sit next to you. Help her get regulated by empathizing with her emotion and modeling self-regulation. Perhaps teach her a calming technique like deep breathing. When she is calm, tell her again that hitting hurts and she may not hit. If you want to remain at the play date, watch closely and try to intervene before anything escalates to something physical. An ounce of prevention is worth a pound of cure! Remain calm, empathize with what she is feeling, but be firm that hitting is unacceptable and take action immediately. If she hits again, leave the playdate early. Her behavior is signaling a need which should be addressed.

Common Questions Addressed:

If I don't spank, use time-out, or take away toys, what tools do I have to discipline with?

If we want to teach our children that yelling, hitting, and snatching things away are not appropriate behaviors, it's a good idea not to practice those things ourselves. As positive parents, our most valuable tools are the example we set and the connection we have with our children. I cannot stress this enough because it truly is the foundation for positive parenting. If your child feels connected to you, and if you have built that foundation of trust and respect, your child, by nature, will not want to disappoint you, and more importantly, because of that connection and the values instilled through that connection, he will hold himself accountable and not want to undermine his own self-concept.

Your example is also a powerful tool. Children are mirrors that reflect back to us our own attitudes and behaviors. Here is where your accountability comes in. If you swear in front of your children, leave messes everywhere, yell or smack your kids, lie to them or others, or talk disrespectfully to your child or to your spouse, you can expect your child to swear, not tidy his room, yell when he's mad, be aggressive, lie, and talk disrespectfully, and it is not fair to punish him for being like you.

There are many tools available to teach your child in a way that doesn't hurt. Time-in is a good option for toddlers and preschoolers. Problem-solving is the way to go with older children. We will discuss these options more in depth in chapters 12-14.

What about accountability? How does positive parenting teach my child to be accountable?

Genuine accountability comes from within, not an outside force. You cannot control and manipulate your child into being accountable for his actions. He will learn to be accountable through life's natural consequences, with your empathetic limits, and with your loving guidance. If he leaves his bike out and it gets ruined, the consequence is he has no bike. If he throws his favorite toy and breaks it, his favorite toy is broken. *That* is the consequence. If you rush out and buy a new bike or toy, the lesson may be lost. On the other hand, if you punish your child for leaving his bike out or breaking the toy, you're just adding insult to injury. Allow your child to learn the natural lessons, and this will teach accountability. Requiring your child to solve his own problems and right his wrongs also teaches this.

This sounds great, but life is not free of punishments and consequences. If he breaks the law, they won't problem-solve with him, they'll throw him in jail.

This is true, but laws and jails were made for adults who have fully developed brains and the full frontal lobe function of sequential thought and logic. We are talking about children here. We mustn't forget that children are not just tiny adults. Developmentally, they have a long way to go, and the way their brains develop depends largely on how we interact with them. We need to focus more on raising emotionally healthy and responsible children than we do on "keeping kids out of jail," - a reason many parents give for harsh discipline. Emotionally healthy and responsible people generally don't break the law and end up behind bars, but our goal isn't just to keep them out of trouble but to to give them the best start possible for a rewarding and happy life.

How will my child know to stay within the boundaries if there isn't a punishment for stepping outside them?

Simply put, the answer is because you will teach her how to live within the boundaries. This is exactly where the entire shift in the parenting paradigm occurs. We are habituated to train children to follow rules by punishing them when they break the rules. Positive parents take a more proactive approach and teach children how to behave well and stay within the limits. It's about teaching them to do what's right rather than punishing them for doing what's wrong.

To illustrate what I mean by this, I'll give two examples of behavior issues many parents tell me they struggle with.

Not listening – or more accurately, not minding – is a common behavior issue that children typically get punished for. Let's say that six-year-old Dalton has trouble getting out the door on school mornings. Many mornings are spent yelling or nagging at Dalton to hurry up and get ready. Out of frustration, a parent might threaten to take away his video game privileges if he doesn't make it to the bus on time. A positive parent would proactively be teaching Dalton the morning routine from an early age and set him up for success. She'd make a visual pocket chart of all of his morning duties for him to complete and move to the "done" pocket so that he can see what is next. She'd have his toothbrush and toothpaste lying within reach and teach him to lay his clothes out the night before. He does this routine consistently for months or even years before he starts school. She empowers him by showing him how to choose appropriate clothing, how to get dressed, how to brush his teeth, where to find his lunch and backpack, etc. When school starts, this is already a regular routine, and because she's spent many months teaching him how to do it independently, there's no scrambling in frustration to make him learn it now. Put the work in teaching a child before it has a chance to become a behavior problem.

Example number two is in regard to aggressive behavior. When Dad sees four-year-old Emily getting upset, he names her emotion and teaches her how to breathe through it. He teaches her ways to handle frustration, like clapping, walking away, jumping, or taking giant dinosaur breaths. He's given her a soothing place with a pillow, blanket, stuffed animal, and books to go to when she's feeling mad to calm herself down. He helped Emily understand and deal with her anger before she hit someone.

Sometimes, of course, there are consequences to actions, and this also helps children understand boundaries, such as the example of leaving the bike out and losing the bike. Consequences are discussed further in chapter 13.

3
Changing Your Mindset

Parenting, like life, is all about perspective.

The way we were raised and our experiences throughout life have wired our brains to certain beliefs and habits. We perform them often at an unconscious level, carrying on the actions and tone of our parents, whether it is good or bad. However, because so many of us were raised with spanking and punishment, *the shift in our thinking* is the hardest but most important step in embracing positive parenting. Thanks to the great strides in neuroscience research over the past few decades, we know that attachment is best for our children; we know that our interactions with them are wiring their brains[4]; and we know that we can begin to make new neural connections, essentially re-wire our brains and theirs, when we become a more conscious parent.

Making the choice to parent gently and respectfully is a wonderful first step, but until you change your mindset, you will find positive parenting challenging, particularly if you were raised punitively. You are essentially re-wiring your own brain to think about children and parenting in a different way.

When you are new to positive parenting, it is common to ask "what do I do instead?" Even if you've read all the "how to" articles, it may not click until you truly change from a fear-based mindset to a love-based mindset.

The fear-based mindset says:

1. I have to control my child's behavior.
2. My child learns through consequences and/or punishment to not repeat bad behavior.
3. I am the dominant figure; my child is under me.

It is possible to be in a fear-based mindset and try to practice positive parenting, which will generally result in trying a nicer approach to the same methods of control (I learned this the hard way) rather than addressing underlying needs and focusing on teaching better behavior. Also, failing to set and enforce limits or correct the child at all is permissiveness and also stems from a fear-based mindset; fear that your child will not like you or your rules.

Do you:

- Use counting to change behavior?
- Use time-outs to change behavior?
- Spank to change behavior?
- Find that, since you don't know how to make your kids mind without punishment, you just don't bother to set real limits, or, because you know now how important relationship is in positive parenting, you try to never put strain on your relationship?
- Set no limits or do not enforce limits because you want your child to like you?

To really make positive parenting work, you need to switch from a fear-based mindset to a love-based mindset. The love-based mindset says:

1. My role is to guide and teach my child appropriate behavior.
2. My child learns through the examples set in the home and through the limits that are set and enforced respectfully and with empathy.
3. While I am the leader, my child has equal rights to be respected and to be heard.

Once you switch to love-based thinking, *what to do instead* will become much more clear and simple.

Tips to help make the shift:
Educate yourself on the development of your child's brain. Understanding what your child is cognitively capable of will go a long way in changing your perspective on behavior.

Re-frame your thoughts surrounding your child's behavior. Instead of seeing it as misbehavior, see it as an opportunity. I know this is easier said than done, but all things get easier with practice. Her behavior may be an opportunity for connection, for teaching a new skill, or for setting a new limit. Her misbehavior could be telling you many things (she's tired, she's bored, she's feeling afraid, she's feeling disconnected).

For example, many parents struggle with tantrums and feel the child needs to be disciplined or ignored during this time. Tantrums are not bad behavior. Tantrums are an expression of emotion that became too much for the child to bear. No punishment is required. What your child needs is compassion and safe, loving arms to unload in. Yes, it may be inconvenient or even embarrassing in the grocery store, but your child is your first priority, not the judgments of onlookers.

So often, children are punished for being human. Children are not allowed to have grumpy moods or bad days. We expect them to be in complete control of their emotional reactions at all times, yet how many of us can do this? Have you never yelled or slammed a door in anger? Have you never snapped at your child or spouse after a stressful day? Have you never given a hateful glare or complained about everyday frustrations? If you have never done those things, then you are certainly entitled to expect your child to be a perfect human, but for the rest of us, for all of us who sometimes slip up, we need to offer the same understanding and grace we hope is afforded to us. We all have hard days. Bad days don't make us bad people. None of us are perfect, and we shouldn't hold our children to a standard of perfection that we ourselves cannot attain.

This is not to say, of course, that you do not correct a disrespectful remark or a sour mood that is disrupting the peace of the home. It is our job to teach our children what is appropriate. Teach them that it's not okay to project a bad mood on those around them. Teach them how to handle frustration, anger, fear, sadness, and disappointment. Teach them that it's not acceptable to be rude to people. High standards are good. Hold them to a high standard! But please, hold yourself to one, too. Don't project your bad moods. Learn how to handle your frustration, anger, fear, sadness, and disappointment. Don't be rude to them. Set the example. We all need high standards, and do you know what else we all need?

A little grace.

You know better, but sometimes you have a bad day and you say something that isn't nice, or you slam a door, or you yell at your kids. We aren't robots. Sometimes life is just plain hard, and we need a break, not a lecture. We need a hug, not a scornful look. We know we did wrong, but we're having a hard time. We need someone who understands. We need someone who still believes in us. We just need grace.

The same goes for our children.

Begin with the end in mind. Look at the big picture and think of the qualities you want your child to have in adulthood. When you are able to look past the now, you can see how the little things don't matter as much as they seem to at the moment, and this perspective helps you to better guide your child.

Parenting is a journey. It is a time of growth, not only for our children, but for us as well. Sometimes we're not sure which path to take, and sometimes in our journey, we get lost and realize we've gone the wrong way. Luckily, it's never too late to turn around and find the right path. My experience is that, when you go down the path labeled **love**, it always takes you where you want to go.

4
Embrace the Seasons

Parenthood has many seasons. As is often our nature, we are regularly looking toward the next season rather than fully embracing and enjoying the one we're in. It's currently winter here – my least favorite season. I'm longing for the sunshine and warmth of spring. Of course, on those blistering hot summer days, I was longing for the chill of winter air. Winter always gives way to spring. Babyhood gives way to toddlerhood. Things are constantly changing, and one of the great keys to joy in life and in parenthood is learning to embrace the season that you're currently in instead of looking to the one ahead.

I remember the exhausting days when I had a two year old and a newborn. My two year old still wasn't sleeping through the night, and my newborn only slept for a couple of hours at a time. I had a toddler in my bed and a newborn in a bedside crib, and some nights I wasn't sure if I had even found sleep. I found myself doing a lot of wishing....

I wish they'd sleep through the night.
I wish they'd sleep in their own room.

I wish I didn't have to lie with them while they fall asleep.
I wish I'd never started co-sleeping.
I wish they were out of diapers.
I wish I had some time for myself.

Now, my babies are big boys. They are out of my bed, out of my room, and long out of diapers. They almost never wake me at night. They sleep in their own room. They don't need me to lie down with them anymore. I give them a kiss and walk out the door – and I have lots of time for me now.

Some nights, I walk out of their room, go curl up in my bed in front of the fire with a good book and think, "Ah. This is nice."

But then there are the other nights when I lie there and listen to them talking with each other (their room is adjacent to mine). I listen as they tell funny stories and belly laugh at each other, and their laughter makes me smile through my tears. Silent tears are falling on my pillow as I stare at my ceiling, remembering the days when they used to need me. They need me less now. And as much I used to wish for "me time" back then is as much as I'm wishing now for "baby time." Once more, I find myself doing a lot of wishing...

I wish they still needed me to lie down with them.
I wish I could hold them all night like I used to.
I wish we were still co-sleeping.
I wish they were back in diapers.
I wish I could still rock them.
I wish I could go back and do it all again, and savor every moment, committing it all to memory, rather than wishing it away.

Time teaches us many lessons. Another valuable lesson time has taught me is to not sweat the small things. Children are unique individuals, yet we try to put them all on the same time line. We expect them to be crawling, walking, talking, potty trained, and reading by a certain age, and we can get our stomach in knots worrying if and why they're missing the mark.

My firstborn was potty trained by age two and a half. It took literally one day. He never looked back. He stayed dry through the night immediately. It was extremely easy. I thought I was a pro.

Son number two set me straight on the whole "pro" idea. He was well into age 4 before he decided to use the potty, and for many, many months after that, he had frequent accidents. I thought he'd go to college in diapers.

Then one day I realized I couldn't remember the last time he had an accident in his undies. Just like that, it ended. I don't know when it happened. All of that worrying was for nothing. That's how these things often go – you think the stage or season will never end, and then suddenly you realize that it has. So, when I begin to worry that my son isn't reading as well at this age as many of his peers, I stop my worrying thoughts and remind myself that he'll get it in his own time.

Childhood is not a race. Neither is parenthood. Let's stop rushing through, looking only for the next season to come, and take time to savor the one we are in. The sand is slipping through the hourglass, and there is no slowing it down. Just a blink, and suddenly there is a bit less in the top of the glass than there was before.

Time is slipping away.

Although time cannot be slowed, it can be embraced. There is delight to be found in our ordinary days. Lifelong relationships are being built in these ordinary days. Your legacy is forged in these ordinary days. While they may pass by seemingly uneventful and unimportant, there is no such thing as an unimportant day when you are shaping a child's life. Something was written on their hearts today – something important. Be intentional about what it is you are writing.

Embrace the time you have. Enjoy the season you are in.

Each season is sweet in it's own way, and each one will be missed when it is gone. Don't miss the beauty of the bud while you're waiting for the blossom. Each stage of a child's life offers us a chance to know him a little better and to grow a little closer. Each stage also gives us a chance to grow into a better parent as we learn the lessons they teach us about loving unconditionally, living wholeheartedly, and giving and receiving grace.

Slow Down, Time

Once my tiny newborn baby,
Now my little man.
You're growing up too fast for me.
Please slow down if you can.

Each day I wish would linger,
But they're gone in a flash.
Each night I hold you tightly
Praying for this to last.

My heart fills with pride
With each new step you take,
But watching time pass quickly
Also causes it to ache.

So, I make the most I can
Of this time when you are small,
Cherishing each and every day
For they're the best days after all.

And I pray when you are older,
That you look back fondly, too,
On the days when you were little
And know how much I love you.

5
Peace Starts with You

Before you had a child, you likely had a predictable flow to your daily life. Sleeping, eating, showering – these were things done on your own terms and in your own time. You also probably had a hobby, something that brought you joy and peace, that relaxed and centered you.

When a child comes into our lives, it is the greatest blessing we are given. It also turns our lives upside down. We eat, sleep, and shower on the baby's terms. We put their needs ahead of ours, and because young infants and toddlers have so many needs, we rarely find time to meet our own. Trying to meet the constant demands of another is tough when we have so little left of ourselves to give. Scrambling to get a shower every day means our leisurely hobbies usually become a thing of the past. Eventually, sleep-deprived and exhausted, we endure an emotional and physical distress that may lead us to behave regrettably.

For a long time, I thought putting my needs at the top of the list was a selfish thing to do. *It's not about me anymore*, I told myself. While that was noble of me, it left me in a poor state of health. It became difficult to see the delight in the ordinary days.

Books and articles told me to get up a few hours before my children and have a lovely cup of coffee and relax. That isn't so easy when you're co-sleeping. If I got up, they got up.

Once you put your children to bed, enjoy time with your spouse or time to yourself for knitting or reading, they said. Ha! Putting my children to bed meant I stayed with them, snuggling and telling stories until they finally fell asleep, and usually I fell asleep there, too. If I did manage to stay awake during the hour or more that it took them to fall asleep, I was so drowsy and exhausted by day's end that there wasn't much left of me. I certainly didn't have the energy or desire to knit.

No matter the sleeping arrangement your family has, I expect you have a similar situation – very little time or energy left over for you, or for your partner. I have good news for you though, tired parent. It doesn't take a lot of time or energy to sustain you through these tiresome days. Here are some practical, achievable tips for refilling your cup and keeping your relationship with your spouse or partner from taking a nosedive.

1. Renew your mind daily. This is crucial. You don't need an hour alone in the morning before children arise. What you need is a reminder that this is but a season and some words of encouragement to uplift you throughout your days. My own renewal is in the form of a notebook which contains my mission statement as a mother – what my goals are in raising my children, what I want them to remember, what I hope to achieve, etc. My notebook contains encouraging and positive quotes I've collected from all over - quotes that remind me of my purpose and quotes that humor me. It also contains a gratitude section. Each day, I jot down at least 3 things I'm grateful for. Intentionally focusing on my blessings restores my perspective. Lastly, my notebook holds "exquisite moments." When my son brings me a handful of dandelions from the yard, I write it down. When one of my children say something that melts my heart, it goes in my exquisite moments section. Exquisite moments are moments I never want to forget. They are the moments that fill my heart.

It only takes a few minutes at a time to renew your mind. Periodically throughout the day, read your mission, jot down your blessings, record your exquisite moments. We may not have large blocks of time in the early season of parenthood, but we have small bits.

When I became intentional about renewing my mind daily, I found that there were several little things I could cut out in my day. When I added it up, plenty of my time was squandered on social media, so now, rather than reaching for my phone to check my newsfeed, I reach for my notebook and renew my mind. It makes a world of difference.

2. Renew your relationship daily. I asked my husband what it is that men need to sustain them in a relationship. His answer might surprise you. "We want to feel appreciated, and we want to make you proud." Take just a couple of minutes to send a sweet text. Wink at him across the dinner table or the changing table. Stop him in his tracks and say, "I know I'm so busy with the baby right now, and I don't always make time to tell you this, but I want you know how much you mean to me and this family. I love you. I appreciate everything you do for us." Words sow seeds in hearts. This is true for our children as well as for partners. Sow seeds of love and appreciation, and that is what you will reap when the harvest comes.

Moms, men also like to know you find them attractive, and they crave intimacy. Don't let this important part of your relationship fall away. You both could use the oxytocin surge. There is at least always time for a long kiss and a shoulder rub. Be loving, tender, and affectionate, and your love will thrive.

Dear men, women's needs aren't much different from yours. She wants to feel loved, appreciated, and attractive. I feel loved when my husband does my laundry or sends me a text to tell me I'm beautiful. What makes your woman feel loved? I feel appreciated when my husband says, "The house smells nice. Thank you." When he acknowledges my efforts, I feel appreciated. I feel attractive when he hugs me for an extra long time when he gets home and says, "Wow, look at you." These are quick and simple antidotes to a strained relationship.

3. Post reminders everywhere. You know the kind of parent and person you want to be. Post reminders of that vision all around your home, in the places you frequent. I have a poem on my bathroom mirror that reminds me to be present with my children. I have a small card in my car sun visor that reminds to not to yell. I wear a bracelet every single day that reminds to give *only love today* (ordered at handsfreemama.com). I have baby pictures posted on the refrigerator, and my mind renewal notebook is never far away. Visual cues help us stay on track. They remind us of our purpose.

Renewing your mind and your relationships will help you feel more peaceful and content. When you feel peaceful, you can give peace to others, and that, my friend, is how peace in the home begins.

6

Own Your Feelings and Actions

Learning to effectively manage our own emotions and actions is crucial. We simply cannot guide our children to self-discipline if we do not possess self-discipline ourselves. If we cannot control our anger outbursts, our anxiety, our fearfulness, and our reactivity, how are we going to teach our children how to do these things?

Many of us never learned how to properly manage our own emotions. As children, we were taught to either stuff them down or blame them on someone else, or probably both. As a result, few parents take ownership of their feelings and actions.

When we say, "You're going to make me spank you if you keep acting like this!" or "you're making me so angry right now! Go to your room!" we are admitting that we don't have control over our own feelings and actions, that our child has control over us. This is a double-edged sword. First, this makes children feel responsible for *our* emotions, and that is a big burden to bear for a child. Second, we're teaching them to play the blame game and not take ownership of their emotions and behaviors as well. "She made me do it!"

"I didn't want to get in a fight at school, but he made me so mad!" This is a cycle that needs to end with us.

The first step to learning how to manage ourselves is to take ownership for our own emotional reactions. Instead of, "You're making me so angry," try "I'm feeling angry right now, and I need to calm down." Don't blame your feelings on anyone else; they are your own. Your child is not responsible for your triggers. You are responsible for understanding why certain things trigger you and then disabling that trigger.

Most often, triggers are formed in us during our early years. For example, if whining triggers an emotional upset in you, it is likely that you were shamed or scolded for whining when you were a child. If crying is a trigger, you may have been told to "quit crying" as a child. If back talk is a trigger, look at what happened when you talked back as a child.

It is helpful to identify your triggers by making a journal. Write down what triggers you, try to find out why it is a trigger for you, and then develop an antidote. Usually, our triggers come with negative thought patterns. "My kid is such a crybaby! He cries over everything!" These negative thought patterns just fuel frustration and build negative feelings. An antidote is a positive thought to replace the negative one that accompanies your trigger. "My child is having a hard time and needs my help." Re-framing the problem in this way will help reduce negative feelings. Over time, if you consistently replace the trigger thought with the antidote thought, this will deactivate your trigger, and this will help you respond to your child rather than react.

Here are some ways to deal with anger in the moment:

1. Choose a mantra to say to yourself (or out loud) when you are angry with your child. Examples may be "I am capable of remaining calm" or "I am safe, there is no emergency." I find it helpful to repeat the beginning of a children's book I always read to mine when they were infants. This brings back feelings of warmth and calm to me.

2. Do something physical. Splash cold water on your face. Jog in place. Put on some music and dance. Get outside for some fresh air.

3. If you feel the need to yell, use a loud, silly voice or make a "toot toot" noise while cupping your mouth with your hands. Don't worry about looking silly to your kids. They'd rather see you look silly than look

scary.

4. If you are prone to lashing out and striking your child when you are angry, walk away immediately. If your child follows you and you continue to be triggered, you may need to go into a room and shut the door for a few seconds, breathe deeply, and repeat your mantra. If you have the self-control, you can release the need for physical contact by saying "I love you" and giving your child a big hug, or if your child isn't opposed to tickling, give her a small tickle on her tummy. This will calm your brain, and the loving physical contact will connect you to what is important. Each time you walk away or hug instead of hit, you are strengthening your new neural connection and pruning away your old pathway that caused you to lash out. If you have serious trouble with striking your child, seek professional help.

5. A gentle answer turns away wrath. Whether you're religious or not, this Proverb is a powerful truth. It's going to take a load of self-control on your part, but if you practice gentleness at all times, it will be easier to respond with gentleness when your child grates your nerves. Speak in soft tones to your children, significant other, and others throughout the day. Think gentle thoughts. Gently touch loved ones - tender hugs, a touch on the shoulder while you speak, a rub on the

head as one passes by.

6. Expand the space. In between every action and reaction, there is a space. Usually the space is extremely small because we react so quickly, but take notice of that space and expand it. Be aware in that space that you have a choice to make. You can choose how to respond, and choose wisely, because the next step you take will teach your child how to handle anger and could either strengthen or damage your relationship.

There are other emotions that we project onto our children besides our anger, and we need to be conscious of those as well. We often project fear, anxiety, even sadness and negativity. Again, these are our emotions to deal with, not our family's. We need to take ownership of them and then deal with them appropriately before they affect those we love. That's not to say we can't confide in our spouse or a friend and ask for help, and it's also not to say that our children can't ever see us feeling worried or angry. That would be superhuman. Indeed, showing our children *how to handle* a full range of emotions is healthy as it teaches them valuable lessons about how to handle their own. The key is showing them *how to handle them*, not *how to wallow in them*.

7

Quell the Yell

Yelling is a hot button topic in parenting circles. We don't want to do it, we don't like doing it, and we feel guilty when we do it, yet we feel justified in yelling because we think it's the only way to get our kids to listen.

In the last chapter, I discussed the importance of being able to control your emotional reactions and gave some suggestions on how to keep anger in check. However, I want to focus an entire chapter on yelling because I've found that even positive parents struggle often with it. Therefore, it's important to understand what gets us to that breaking point where we just snap.

Why is this so important? Nearly every parent yells at their kid, so what's the big deal? It's important because one study says that yelling is as harmful as hitting.[5] So, even if you've committed to not raising your hand to your child, raising your voice can still feel like a smack across the face. It's also important because it sets a poor example of communication and because it erodes the connection between parent and child as trust and respect are lost.

Why Do We Yell?

Yelling is a function of the limbic system, the emotional centers of your brain. This is located lower in the brain than your cerebral cortex (your thinking brain) and also houses (in the amygdala) the fight, flight, or freeze response. Here's how it works in a nutshell: Information is always coming at us. It goes through the amygdala first, and the amygdala decides where to send it, either to the cortex or the limbic system. If the incoming information triggers an emotional charge, it gets sent to the limbic system, the more primitive emotions center. Now you're reacting without giving much thought to the consequences (because logic and reasoning take place in the cortex, and you're not there!), so then a flood of hormones is released that causes you to be alarmed. You get a surge of energy, and you release it by yelling.

Why Do We Feel Bad About It?

Once you're brain and body calm down, your cortex reengages, and you can now reason again. Now you feel terrible about yelling at your child because you see it wasn't a reasonable action to take, and the guilt train makes a full stop at your door and invites you in. The guilt train isn't necessarily a bad ride to take, as long as you don't stay on for too long. Guilt can be a good motivator for change if we choose to acknowledge it and create a plan for avoiding such behavior in the future.

Your No-Yell Plan

So, how can you stop your brain from being hijacked the next time your child pours water on the floor? If I had a concrete, one-size-fits-all answer for that question, I'd make millions. Unfortunately, we're all wired a bit differently, so you'll have to find out what works for you, but one of these tips is bound to help you make headway.

1. Join a support group. There are several yell-free groups on social media – just do a search – but if you're uncomfortable letting strangers know your business, gather up a few close friends and enlist their help. Tell them of your plan to yell less at your family, and have them hold you accountable. Reporting your progress to others is a good motivator for many people.

2. Declare the house a yell-free zone. Post signs. Bonus:

The kids can't yell either! I'm generally not a rewards kind of person, but for special cases, I'd say it's quite all right to give yourself a pom pom in a jar every time you manage to quell the yell. When that jar is full, get those new shoes you've been eyeing. You deserve it!

3. Pretend there are cameras all over your house, and someone is always watching. Isn't it amazing how we can manage to keep our cool when company is over or we're in the middle of the grocery store? That's because we know people are watching and judging. If we can control it then, we can control it anytime. So, my friend, fake it until you make it. Pretend there's an audience, and put on a good show!

4. Go to the bathroom when you're feeling the heat rising. It's good to walk away, and this gives you something to go do. Go to your bathroom mirror and yell silently (only mouth what you want to say) at yourself. Why on earth? Well, this does two things. One, you get it out. Sort of. Two, you see exactly what it is that your child sees. That image of the twisted raging mom or dad face is likely to stick with you the next time you feel like blowing a gasket.

5. Be proactive. If you know mornings make you mad, change your morning routine. Once you're familiar

with your triggers, you can avoid a good deal of them.

6. Practice yoga or meditation. I know, who has time for that, right? A few minutes a day can make a big difference, and I'd rather meditate for 15 minutes than feel remorseful for several days.

7. Do you remember your mind renewal book from chapter 5? Grab it and read for several minutes while you take some deep breaths. Your quotes and notations will shift your mood and remind you of your goals.

Sometimes, despite your best effort, you may end up yelling. You're human. Note what made you yell so that you can make a plan for the next time that particular situation arises, apologize to your loved one, tell them it wasn't their fault and that you made a mistake, and then move on. *Move on, sister (or brother).*

8

The Positive Leader

There are those who make the incorrect assumption that positive parents *only* want to "be their child's friend." While it's true that friendship is a part of our role, it is most definitely not the only role. Positive parents are leaders who recognize that children depend on our leadership and guidance. Our leadership is about role modeling, guiding, and protecting.

Letting children lead makes them feel unsafe. No child wants to be the leader; it's too much responsibility for them. They take comfort in knowing that we are in control and capable of taking care of them and managing our homes. This allows them the freedom to just be a child.

How to be a Positive Leader

Children naturally look to their caregivers for leadership. Simply by being loving and attentive, we have shown them over and over again that we are able to meet their needs and provide for them. They instinctively know to look up to us, and will do so unless we manage to sever our connection and push them to attach to peers rather than to us.

Effective leaders:

1. *Set clear boundaries.* Kids need appropriate limits. Permissive parents fail to set and/or enforce limits, but positive parents establish clear boundaries and enforce them consistently and kindly.

2. *Understand that leading and controlling are very different.* Leaders have the ability to elicit cooperation while dictators simply force it.

3. *Are focused.* Leaders know what they intend to accomplish and keep their eyes on the goal. They are intentional about the family environment they create.

4. *Have integrity.* They practice what they preach. They model the behaviors they expect from their children. True authority is not gained through an iron fist but through excellent character.

5. *Are empowering.* Remember the goal is ultimately to raise competent, confident human beings, and that is done in millions of small, empowering moments over childhood. From trusting them enough to take off the training wheels to handing them the keys to get behind the wheel, leaders help their children to feel capable.

6. *Are inspiring.* Leaders foster a positive environment which allows their children to flourish. They know how to bring out the best in everyone.

7. *Show support.* Leaders are encouraging and supportive.

8. *Show confidence.* Leaders believe in themselves and in their ability to lead. (Have faith in yourself! You were chosen for this job for a reason!)

9. *Have a sense of humor.* Don't try to get through 18+ years with children in the home without a sense of humor. Leaders know how to let loose and laugh if off.

10. *Are excellent communicators.* Leaders keep the lines of communication open always. Children have to feel comfortable in talking to the leader about anything without fear.

11. *Are gentle.* The best leaders are gentle. In our culture, we have been misled to believe that the tougher we are, the more respect we will gain, but that is simply not true. What we gain by being tough is fear, and fear is not respect. Respect is gained by giving it away.

The Role of a Friend

You've undoubtedly heard it said, "I'm your parent, not your friend!" That sounds as conflicting to me as "I'm your wife, not your friend!" Why can't I be both? It seems to me that these parents are equating *friend* with *someone who allows you to do stupid things and joins in on the stupidity*. That isn't my definition of friend at all!

Of course we should have a friendship with each of our children. It is that friendship which fosters connection, trust, and cooperation. It is that friendship which will sustain our relationship when they are grown. However, we can't be *just* a friend. I think this is where some parents run into a problem. Our relationship moves beautifully beyond the boundaries of friendship. We are their parents, and being a parent involves more than *just* friendship. It means we are their example, their teacher, and their guide. Being a parent means unconditionality. It means accepting them and loving them for who they are. It means a love and understanding that *just* a friend cannot provide.

Therefore, let us not say "I'm your parent, not your friend!" Let us instead say:

I am you arms when you need a hug.

I am your shoulder when you need to cry.

I am your ears when you need to be heard.

I will pick you up when you fall.

I will cheer you on when you succeed.

I will encourage you when you fail.

Most friends will come and go, but I, my child will never turn my back on you.

You can count on me.

As long as there is breath in me, I am here for you.

I am your friend, and I am so much more.

9
The Playful Parent

Play has many emotional, cognitive, social, physical, and educational benefits. Through play, children release energy, reduce stress, and enjoy life. They learn to problem-solve, exercise creativity, use their imaginations, and master new concepts. Play builds self-confidence, fine and gross motor skills, as well as vocabulary and communication skills. Through play, children learn cooperation, sharing, and conflict resolution. Play matters. Scientists say that play builds a better brain.[6]

For positive parents, play has another vital role – it connects parent and child. When we step into a child's world and play, many opportunities open up. Through the simple act of pausing our adult agendas to be fully present and play, we:

- gain trust
- laugh, releasing tension and stress for all
- learn about the child
- have an opportunity to teach through play
- send the message that the child matters to us

Play is unfortunately being increasingly stripped from

childhood. As the world buzzes and dings constantly around our heads, whirring by at high speed, we are lucky to get everyone bathed and fed, let alone make time for play. After all, there are much more pressing things on our to-do lists.

I encourage you, gentle parent, to put play as a top priority on your to-do list. Positive parenting is built on the parent-child relationship, and play is an excellent relationship builder.

Have you ever heard of disciplining through play? Discipline is teaching, and teaching is best done when the child is open and receptive to listening. A child is never more open and receptive than she is when she is playing. Harness this opportunity to teach values and life skills through pretend play and stories. If there is a recurring issue, it can be brought up gently and safely through acting out the scene in play. For instance, use puppets to show what they would do in a similar situation. By making it silly and fun, the child receives the information and processes it more easily than she would through a lecture or confrontation.

Most of play, however, shouldn't be about teaching lessons. They learn plenty when play is free and child-led. Follow your child into his imaginary world and see where he takes you.

As a mom of just boys, my floor stays covered in LEGO pieces, and I've had many epic Transformers battles. I've spent hours digging in dirt, talking in a pirate's voice, flying into outer space, and even capturing bugs. In other words, I've had to learn a whole new way to play. I've stepped into new territory in order to connect with my boys, and while LEGOs and Transformers don't thrill me, having a good relationship with my children does. The trips to outer space are cool, though, and they've opened up a whole new imaginary world to me, which I love!

The more we play, the more peaceful and happy our home is. Play is therapeutic. We get along better, feel calmer, are closer, and we are all better behaved because we are connected and less stressed when we've taken the time to play together. Be intentional about fitting it in daily and resolve to give your child the gift of a playful parent.

If you need play ideas, see Appendix B. There, you will find 365 of them!

10
Building a Positive Self-Concept

Self-concept can be defined as the view one has of himself and his abilities. A child's self-concept begins to develop at birth with how adults respond to him. Parents and caregivers create a positive emotional bond with an infant through caring interactions with a lot of touch and eye contact.

As the child grows, his ability to interact successfully with his environment promotes a healthy self-concept. This is critically important in early childhood. The development of a positive self-concept at an early age empowers the child to feel competent, try new things, and strive for success. As parents, we have the opportunity (and responsibility) to help our child build a positive self-concept.

How can you tell if a child has a positive or negative self-concept? Children with a positive self-concept exhibit a "can do" attitude. They generally believe in their ability to complete tasks without help, or with minimal help. They do not exhibit problematic behaviors as doing so would be against their positive self-concept.

Children with a negative self-concept exhibit a "can't do" attitude. They become easily frustrated and give up on difficult tasks. These children may exhibit behavior problems if *naughty* or *bad* is a part of their self-concept.

What can parents do to help their children develop a positive self-concept?

Watch the language you use to describe your children. Do not label them with words such as *lazy*, *naughty*, *aggressive*, or *stupid*. Instead, look for and point out your child's strengths.

Provide them with opportunities for success. Give age-appropriate tasks the child can complete on her own. Having done so will give her a sense of pride and help build a "can do" mentality and positive self-concept. Show your children that you have faith in their goodness and in their abilities. This is a matter of language choice. For example, if your toddler, out of frustration, hits another child, you might say, "You naughty girl! How can you be so mean! I can't believe you hit him! You're in big trouble!" Or, you could say, "You got frustrated and hit him. It's not OK to hit. I know you didn't mean to hurt him. How can you express your frustration in different ways? Would you like a stress ball to squeeze?" Which do you think leads to a positive self-concept?

Alternatively, let's use the example that your child is working on a puzzle and is having trouble getting it to fit together properly. If you see frustration building, you might say, "Looks like you can't do that puzzle. Why don't you forget about that one and try something easier?" Or you can offer encouragement and help. "I know you're frustrated. The last time you kept trying and were able to finish it. If you want some help, I'm right here." The first approach tells your child it's OK to quit when it gets hard. The second acknowledges hard work, even if it doesn't result in success the first time.

Competence = Confidence

Parents sometimes think they must point out mistakes and often correct the child in order to make her competent. This is dangerously false. Constant criticism erodes self-confidence as it is always pointing out their failures and weaknesses. When we emphasize what our children do right, however, children will feel good about themselves and continue to strive to meet that positive self-concept.

Giving your child opportunities to do things for himself will help him to develop that "can-do" attitude. Allowing him to dress himself (no matter how mismatched or odd his choices are), putting things within his reach, such as his plates and utensils in a low drawer, clothes hanging on a low rack so that he may choose for himself, and step stools so he may reach the sink himself, will all help aid in making him feel competent, and therefore, confident.

A healthy self-concept is the foundation for the positive development and overall well-being of a child.[7] Because humans behave according to their self-concept, it is crucial to take care in helping your child develop one that is positive. When the self-concept is poor, the potential for poor behavior is fostered. When a child has a healthy self-concept, he sees himself as loved, loving, and valuable, and he will conduct himself in such a manner.

11

The Power of Your Words

There is one whose rash words are like sword thrusts, but the tongue of the wise brings healing. Proverbs 12:18, Holy Bible, ESV[8]

Words are powerful. Words are especially powerful when said by parents to their children. Words have the power to build up and words have the power to tear down.

In the last chapter, it was discussed how the words we use can either foster a positive self-concept or a negative self-concept. We can also foster connection or disconnection, elicit cooperation or rebellion, and hurt or heal, depending on what we allow to come out of our mouths.

Your words sow seeds in the hearts of your children. From those seeds spring up either confidence or uncertainty, dignity or dishonor, worth or worthlessness. Your words create the beginning of their life stories, and they will carry this story with them always. Your words help them understand who they are and what worth they have in this world.

Use words that encourage your child rather than discourage. Encouragement is not the same as praise. Encouragement recognizes his capabilities and expresses faith in your child as he is.

Words that Encourage:

I love to watch you do that!

I have faith in you.

You're doing well.

I see you put a lot of effort into that.

That took courage.

You have a kind heart.

That was very helpful. Thank you.

We all make mistakes. It's okay.

You two make a great team!

Words that Discourage:

Don't color outside the lines again.

That's probably too hard for you.

You can do better that that!

All you ever do is whine.

Is that really the best you can do?

You're never going to get this.

Nagging, demanding, and lecturing typically have the opposite effect we are going for. Speaking in a firm, assertive, kind voice at a relational distance elicits cooperation much more quickly. Think of how you like to be asked to do something. Are you more likely to comply joyfully if someone barks a command at you or asks you politely?

Words that Elicit Cooperation:
Please clean your room by noon today.
I would appreciate your help with the yard work today.
Thank you for putting the dishes away.
Please help me clean up the playroom, and I'll help you tidy your bedroom.
I noticed your room was already clean. You're very responsible.

Words that Elicit Rebellion:
You never pick your clothes up off the floor!
Your room is always a pigsty!
Get in there and clean that room right now!
If you don't pick up your toys, I'm throwing them all in the trash!

Words can also create contention in the family. Comparing a child to a sibling serves no purpose but to create sibling rivalry and hurt feelings. Think how you would feel if your child said, "Elijah's mom lets him do it." What is your first reaction? "Well, I'm not Elijah's mom!" People do not like to be compared unfavorably. It damages self-esteem and puts us on the defensive. Children are people, too. By the same token, our words can create peace. By valuing each child for who he or she is and noting their positive qualities – by speaking out the greatness we see in each person in our home – we foster contented hearts. Contented hearts are hearts at peace.

Do you remember cutting words spoken to you in a moment of anger by a loved one? Remember how they still hurt months and even years later. Do you remember words being spoken to you that seemed to wrap you in a hug and brought healing?

Let's use our words to speak life over our children. May our words uplift their souls, heal their hearts, mend broken spirits, and encourage them to try again. Let your words cover your child in love and grace.

Words that Heal:
I love you, no matter what.
I'm proud to be your parent.
You're an important part of this family.
I will always be here for you.

Words that Hurt:

Why can't you be more like your brother?

You're such a crybaby!

I'm so disappointed in you.

You make things so difficult.

Four Little Words:

There are 4 words that a child should hear regularly. These 4 simple words will take root in a child's heart and bless him his entire life.

I believe in you.

When your child is facing something difficult, "You will overcome this. *I believe in you.*"

When your child is successful, "I knew you could do it. *I believe in you.*"

When your child has made a mistake, "You'll make this right. *I believe in you.*"

When we believe in them, they learn to believe in themselves, and that is a priceless gift to give them. We all long to have at least one person in our corner, no matter what, who we know believes the best in us. A parent should be that one person (or two)!

Other words that plant positive seeds which will spring forth self-worth in your child's heart:

I see you.

In the age of busyness and distractions, our children need to know that we see them, truly *see them.*

"I see you bringing a drink for your sister."
"I see you taking good care of your things."
"I see you swinging high."
"I see you doing your best on your homework."

Childhood is so fleeting, and although, in the thick of busy days and restless nights, it seems it will drag on forever, the reality is it will be over all too soon. Ask any parent of grown children how quickly it happens. Leave the distractions behind for a while each day and just *look.*

You matter.

"You matter more than the mess."
"You matter more than the phone."
"You matter more than the broken vase."
"You matter more than my inbox."

When you've had one call after another and your little one is tugging on your shirt, remember what really matters. When the milk is splattered all over the floor and those little eyes are looking at you for your reaction, remember what really matters. It takes a few minutes to clean up spilled milk; it takes much longer to clean up a broken spirit.

I believe in you.
I see you.
You matter.

Tell them often and watch them flourish.

12

Teaching Tools

Discipline doesn't mean to punish. The root word is disciple, which means to *teach*. We are not focusing on busting bad behavior but on teaching what is moral and acceptable. There are many ways to teach a child. Here are some tools that I have found to be useful over the years.

Modeling

This is so, so important. Behave the way you want your children to behave. They learn by watching your example! Let them see you being compassionate and kind. Speak to them respectfully. Each interaction with your child is teaching her something. If you want her to learn not to interrupt you in conversation, model by not interrupting her when she speaks as well. If you want him to use his manners, use yours. When you yell at your kids, you teach them to yell. Adversely, when you speak gently, you teach them to do the same.

Play

Play is vital to childhood. Children learn openly through play. I believe this is when they learn best! Their brains are engaged, receptive, absorbing everything! This is a wonderful opportunity to not only connect with your child, but to teach valuable lessons! Here are some ideas to teach through play:

-Make a Game

One idea is to make a manners box game. One box is used for appropriate behaviors, and the other for inappropriate behaviors. Write down several behaviors/manners on stars, and let your child choose which box to put each star in.

-Puppet Shows

It doesn't have to be a big production. Make some sock puppets if you'd like. Use the puppets to act out a scene and teach a lesson. This can also be done with toys. You can use bears, dolls, or whatever you'd like and act out different scenes. Kids really do listen and absorb lessons through play!

-Role Playing

Be your child, and let your child be you. Show her what is appropriate in certain situations. We have role-played eating at a restaurant, how to sit quietly in a class, and how to handle various situations. The kids have a blast, and it helps them to remember!

-Daily Words

We have a daily word that I post on the refrigerator. I explain the meaning and we will act out what it means. This not only builds vocabulary, but words such as empathy and gratitude teach wonderful values!

-Story Time
Of course there are lots of children's books that teach morals and manners, but we like to make up our own stories here, too! My youngest prefers to look through books, but my oldest really likes to listen to made-up stories. This is a wonderful opportunity to teach cause and effect. They're listening!

Visuals

A fun way to teach your child responsibility is to make a visual chart. There are no rewards associated; this is purely a visual reminder. These charts remind children so YOU don't have to! Be creative! Get your child involved in making the chart. You can clip pictures from magazines or use pictures of your child doing various activities to glue to the chart. Visual reminders can also help children become more organized and independent.

Social Interactions

A day at the park, a few hours at the library, playdates

with friends, *life IS learning*. What if your child witnesses another child being inappropriate? This is an opportunity for you to talk about what happened and teach appropriate behaviors.

Empathy

Teaching our children emotional intelligence is an important part of parenting. We must accept all of our children's feelings. This doesn't mean we must accept all the behaviors that come with them, of course. We must teach healthy ways to channel those feelings, but ALL feelings are acceptable. Being empathetic with your child will help him regulate his big emotions, like fear and anger, more quickly and model for him how to be empathetic with others.

Family Meetings

Family meetings are wonderful tools that bring the entire family together to talk about family events and issues in a comfortable, connecting way. Family meetings make children feel like integral members of the family unit.

If you're not sure what to include in your family meeting, I've included our family meeting schedule below:

1. Appreciations. Each person names something a family member did that week that he or she appreciates.

2. Contributions. This is the distribution of family work. List contributions that need done or put them in a bowl and let kids choose. If they are absent from the meeting or refuse to choose, choose for them. Be consistent with follow through. If they don't like the job they drew, explain they can pick another one in 7 days.

3. Problem-solving and planning. Tackle any problems on the agenda (kids can add to the agenda, too). If there are no problems on the agenda for the week, work on vacation or weekend planning.

4. Allowances. If you give your children an allowance, the end of the family meeting is a nice time to hand those out.

Tips for successful family meetings:

1. Have the meeting at the same time, same place every week if possible.

2. Keep the meeting between 15 and 20 minutes. Start and end on time so kids don't get bored and so they know the meeting is consistent.

3. Treat family meetings with respect and hold them at the table.

4. Start an appreciation board in your home. This could be a small dry erase board centrally located. This helps children to watch for and point out things they appreciate other family member's doing. An example on the board might be, "I appreciate Jane for making my bed for me."

5. Start an agenda board as well. This board includes all upcoming events such as birthday parties and vacations and also is a place to write problems to be discussed at the meeting. The agenda board should not be a tattling board, but a "no name, no blame" board where children and adults in the family can write issues they are having. Discuss everything on the agenda for the week at the meeting. If the family cannot come to a consensus on a problem, it "stays on the table." Parents give a solution until the family comes to consensus. Revisit it next week to see if the parents' solution works for everyone or if they'd like to put it back on the table for discussion. Everyone must commit to solving the

problem.

Consequences and Problem-Solving

See Chapter 13.

13
Consequences and Problem-Solving

"Rules rarely keep us in line. Love does a much better job at keeping us moral." - Dr. Henry Cloud [9]

Whether you're new to positive parenting or a seasoned veteran, the issue of consequences can get your head spinning. Logical and natural, positive and negative consequences; what is the difference between them all?

A logical consequence is related to the behavior but is imposed by someone else; it does not come naturally. For example, if your child throws a toy at someone, it is logical to take that toy away. The problem with logical consequences is that they often get twisted into punishment. When logical consequences are delivered with empathy and as a form of teaching, they are useful; however, when they are used to make the child "pay" for the wrongdoing and are not accompanied with a teaching moment, this becomes a punishment. Your *intent* is the key as to whether the consequence becomes a useful teaching tool or is turned into merely a punishment.

Natural consequences occur as a natural result of the

child's choice without any intervention from parents or caregivers. An example would be, if your child refuses to wear a coat in the winter, he will get cold. Being cold is the natural consequence of not wearing a coat.

Positive consequence is generally a term used to describe praise or rewards.

A negative consequence simply means the child experiences something negative as a result of his behavior.

I'm going to attempt to simplify this whole consequence confusion and help you avoid the pitfall of turning a teaching consequence into punishment by giving you one secret tool.

Replace the idea of giving consequences with the idea of problem-solving.

Do you see how this changes the whole concept in your mind? Now it's not about coming up with something to do *to* your child, it's about working *with* your child to find a solution. Having your child involved in the problem-solving process will not only teach him valuable lessons and instill self-discipline, but it will leave his dignity intact, and he'll feel good about himself and his relationship with you.

Let me give you just a couple of examples of problem-solving instead of imposing consequences.

Note: Because problem-solving is a prefrontal cortex function, the child probably won't be ready to be involved in the problem-solving process until at least age 4. However, you can certainly let your younger-than-4 children hear you problem-solve. Talk it through with them. "You wanted Emma's doll, so you took it from her, but now Emma is crying. You both want the doll. How can we solve this problem? How about you and Emma take turns with the doll?"

Scenario
Your 5 year old son gets upset at Grandma's house and yells "I don't like you!" to her. Grandma tells you about it when you pick him up. Instead of telling him he was rude and taking away his TV for 2 days, you can involve him in making it better.

Ask him what happened at Grandma's. Hear him out. You might say, "I understand you got upset. Everyone gets upset sometimes, but we have to be careful with words because they can hurt. Do you think those words hurt Grandma's feelings?" Ask him, "How can we make Grandma feel better? Can you think of something?" He may decide to pick her some flowers or make her a card or write her an apology note. If he doesn't come up with anything on his own, offer him a few suggestions like I just listed and let him choose. When he chooses, help him carry out his solution by taking him outside to pick the flowers or giving him supplies to make a card.

The lesson: He has learned that his words have power and he should use them carefully. He has also learned that he must right his wrongs himself and that he is not absolved with a simple time-out.

Scenario

Your 13-year-old has math homework due the next day, but she wants to go to a movie with her friend. You remind her of the homework, and she says, "I hate homework! I want to go to the movie!" Resist the urge to make her sit down and do it *this instant* and give her an opportunity to problem-solve. You might say, "Well, I'd rather watch a movie than do homework too, but I wonder what your teacher will say if you don't have your homework?" Lend an empathetic ear to what she has to say. If she doesn't begin to come up with a solution, you can coach her. "What time does the movie start? I'll bet you can get the homework done in time and still make the movie, and you'll have your homework ready for your teacher tomorrow."

The lesson: Time management is *her* responsibility, as is her school work.

Obviously every scenario can go a hundred different ways, but the idea is to involve your child in the process. Let your child come up with as much of the solution with as little prompting from you as possible, but do offer coaching if he's young or having a difficult time problem-solving himself. There should be no shaming, blaming, or anger in the problem-solving process. If your child is upset, or if you are, wait until everyone is calm to begin the process. If your child completely refuses to be involved in the problem-solving process, then it may be appropriate to go ahead and talk it through yourself -- out loud-- to model this, and then come up with your own solution, but remember to do so with the intent of *teaching* and not punishing. It may also be appropriate to allow the natural outcome to occur instead. For example, in scenario 2, if she had chosen the movie over homework, let her face the teacher without her homework and be held accountable for her choice.

14

Enforcing Limits Versus Punishments

"Power is of two kinds. One is obtained by the fear of punishment and the other by acts of love. Power based on love is a thousand times more effective and permanent than the one derived from fear of punishment." - Mahatma Gandhi [10]

Limits are imperative and it is important to set them and enforce them. Positive parents are not doormat parents, nor are we permissive. I realize that the lines between enforcing limits and giving consequences or punishments get blurry. If you look at anything hard enough, it can be viewed as a punishment. It is easy to over-think it and get caught up in the semantics. The key, again, is *your intent*. Positive parenting does not mean that our kids will never experience consequences for their actions. Some actions have negative consequences; that is just life, and it's an important lesson to learn. What's important is how those consequences are experienced by the child. Again, it is always better to come up with a solution that empowers your child to learn self-discipline and make amends than it is to simply dish out an arbitrary consequence.

If our goal is to make the child feel guilty, we end up focusing him on his inadequacy. This causes the child to either feel bad about himself or to blame others for being mean in an attempt to defend himself against feeling bad. Neither of these inspire him to reflect on his actions.

Dr. Becky Bailey says, "To govern himself, a child needs to know how he feels, not what his parents think he should feel. To teach, we should focus on what we want our child to reflect upon, what we want him to learn, and also take into account the aspects of our child that we want to highlight. Then we can deliver the consequence with the intent of teaching. More often than not, problem-solving is the better course to take as this will involve him the process of righting wrongs and foster self-discipline."[11]

Let's ask the big question! What do I do when my kid breaks my limit if I don't punish? Here are some examples.

Limit: No throwing toys in the house.
Scenario: Your preschooler just hurled a truck clear across the room, narrowly missing brother's head. Pick up the truck and say, "Whoa! You threw this truck

really far! Remember, you may not throw toys in the house." Hand the child the toy back. Say, "If you throw again, we'll have to put the toy up." If he plays nicely with it, great. If he throws it again, say, "Oops, let's put this toy away for now. We'll try again later." *Smile* "Let's color!"

Taking the toy was not a punishment; you were enforcing your limit. You didn't take it in anger. You kept your tone kind. You didn't shame him or call him naughty. You engaged him in another activity. Your *intention* was not to make him feel guilty but to teach him what is appropriate. Now, if he gets mad that you put the toy up, you will *empathize* with his upset. "I see you're upset about the toy. We'll try that toy again later. When you're feeling better, we'll color!"

Or, let's say it's a nice, warm day out. You could say, "Whoa, you threw this truck really far! Remember, you may not throw toys in the house. Would you like to go outside and throw a ball?" If he says "yes," let him throw to his heart's desire out there. If he refuses to go out and you give him the toy again and he throws it again, repeat the above steps.

Limit: Food stays on the table.

Scenario: Your toddler is at the table eating lunch. Suddenly, you are smacked right in the cheek with a carrot. One option is to sing a funny song. In a singing voice, "Silly girl, I know you're able to keep your food on the table!" If nothing else, she'll giggle and forget to throw the food. Humor can be a powerful parenting tool, but we'll get to that later. If she throws it again, you might say, "You're throwing your food, you must not be hungry" and remove the plate. If she cries that she is hungry, I'm a believer in second chances. Sing it again! "Okay silly girl, now I know you're able to keep your food on the table! Eat it up!" If she starts throwing it again, take it back and try again in 30 minutes. The game will soon lose its appeal.

Limit: No hitting.
Scenario: Brother and sister are playing. Things go awry and brother bops sister on the head. Sister comes crying to you. First you tend to sister. Give her cuddles and make sure she's OK. Go to brother, but not with an angry attitude. He might be the aggressor, but he has feelings, too. Kids who *do* bad *feel* bad. Get down on his level; maybe scoop him up in your lap. "You hit your sister and she's hurt. Remember, we don't hit. What happened?" At this point, he may either explain his side or break down crying. If he cries, show him empathy. Bad feelings can make you do bad things. Get

rid of the bad feelings and feel good again and you do better. Once, he's regulated, it's time to problem-solve. If he told you what happened to cause the thump, you have a good starting point. "Hitting hurts. How can you make your sister feel better? What can you do next time so that you don't hit her?" If he's old enough, let him come up with solutions, such as draw her a picture and walk away when he's angry. If he doesn't come up with a solution, offer him ideas. This whole process of him on your lap or close to you could be called a *time-in*. You're showing him the behavior is not allowed and you're helping him to come up with tools to handle it better next time. You're not turning him away or shaming him. Your *intention* is not to make him feel guilty or bad but to teach. This is a win-win.

Limit: No playing video games until homework is done. Scenario: Your 8-year-old has homework, but he asks if he can play a short game and then do it. You say politely, "You know the rule, sweetheart. You may play when your homework is finished."

"But mom!!!!"

"I can see you really want to play that game. It is fun, isn't it? I bet you're close to beating the game now, aren't you?!"

"Yes! And I really want to get started playing!"
"I know you do. How about you get started on your homework while I put some cookies in the oven, then when you're finished, we'll have some cookies and I'll watch you play?"

"Aw. OK."

It may not go that smoothly, obviously. Don't get involved in a power struggle. *State the limit, keep your attitude kind, and stick to it.* If he storms off or says you stink, tell him that was hurtful and you'd appreciate it if he didn't talk to you like that, and let him go storming off. He's not getting to play his game, so there's no need to add something to that. *That* would be retaliation or punishment. Your *intent* then would be to make him feel guilty or bad. Right now, you're being calm, kind, and simply enforcing your limit. When he's calmed down, you can go in and talk to him about the reason for the rule and empathize with his upset about it. He'll eventually decide it's best to get it done so he can play. Once he's done, let him play his game, sit with him, and enjoy each other's company. This is repairing the rift.

Here's the difference.

Punishment is retaliation. The intention of punishment is to make the child feel bad or remorseful for what he did. It is usually not related at all to the behavior and it does not teach alternatives. In scenario #1, if you'd have yelled at the child and taken the toy away for the rest of the day saying, "Fine! You just lost that toy!" then that would have been a punishment. You'd be mad, he'd be feeling crummy. *The intention would have been different.* If ,in #2, you'd have said "If you can't do better than that, you don't get lunch!!!" that would have been a punishment. You'd have been mad, she'd have felt bad. In #3, if you'd spanked him or sent him to his room for hitting his sister, that would have been a punishment. In #4, if you'd taken the game away for the day or a week, that would have been a punishment. Punishment leaves the child feeling bad about himself. It causes a disconnect and doesn't teach a corrective behavior.

Enforcing limits can and should be done kindly and with empathy. In #1, you were kind and gave your child an acceptable alternative (throwing outside), and you engaged with him in another activity, quickly repairing the rift. The limit was enforced, you stayed connected, you both felt good. The same is true for the other scenarios.

If there is a disconnect, as inevitably there will be times when children just do not like our limits or the consequences of their actions, just repair the rift as soon as possible.

The goal in enforcing limits is to teach, leave everyone's dignities intact, and remain connected or reconnect soon after.

15
Restore and Reconnect

Positive parenting rests upon the foundation of connected relationships. However, relationships are never perfect because the people within each relationship cannot be perfect. As a result, sometimes trouble will come our way. Sometimes our relationships will be strained. Disconnects are a normal part of human relationships.

We may find ourselves disconnected because we haven't been intentional at maintaining the relationship.

We may find ourselves disconnected because we've allowed the hectic busyness of life to interfere with our play time.

We may find ourselves disconnected because we, despite our best efforts, yelled or was harsh.

We may find ourselves disconnected because our child, despite his best efforts, made a poor choice.

To find oneself in a disconnected state at times is

normal, but to stay there is nonsense. When we realize that we are in this state of disconnection, it is time to seek to repair it. We cannot wait on our child (or husband or friend) to extend a peace offering first. We must be mature enough to be the first to reach out. That requires us to be vulnerable and courageous. Sometimes it's hard to be the one to apologize first or to admit a wrongdoing, but we are strong.

Restoration is necessary if you have corrected your child for any reason. Restoration simply means that you bring that wayward child back into the fold, back into your loving embrace, and tell her that she is good, that you two are *good*. Correction is necessary in raising children, yet one should always come out on the other side feeling worthy and good. Bad choices don't make us bad people, and children need to believe you see them in a positive light despite their mistakes.

The same is true for you, gentle parent. You need to see your worthiness and goodness even when you've messed up royally. I hope you have someone in your life who reminds you of your goodness. I hope you have *that one person* who always sees your light and encourages you to see it, too. If you don't, you will have to do self-restoration. Show compassion to yourself. Remind yourself of all the times you didn't blow it – all the times you showed up and gave it your all. Then, find yourself *that one person*. Reach out to family, neighbors, friends, church members, and find *that one person*. We all need one.

Once you and your child are restored – feeling worthy, good, and valued – then your hearts are open to reconnect. This reconnection time needs to take precedence over all other things in that moment. Here are some tips for reconnecting with your child:

1. Tune in completely to your child. Leave distractions behind and be completely present and available. Ask if there is anything your child needs to say. Listen intently and respond thoughtfully.

2. Play. This is a wonderful way to reconnect with younger children. Basically, play whatever your child wants to play, let him lead the play as you follow along, and, if possible, let him be the one to end the play time during this reconnection phase.

3. With an older child, you may offer to go out for a dinner date, catch a movie, play board games, or just hang out and spend quality time together.

4. Write a love note. Written word has a way of working

its way down into our souls. That's why we love books so much. Write the contents of your heart out on a piece of paper and leave it on your child's pillow.

5. Keep your word and follow through on promises. If the disconnection was because you were in the wrong, and you tell your child you will try not to do whatever it was again, then really try. When your child sees your effort, you will build trust, and therefore connection.

Keep learning. Keep trying. Keep loving.

16
Ten Alternatives to Punishment

Punishment is often synonymous with discipline, but these are two entirely different things. Punishment, by definition, is the imposition of something negative or unpleasant on a person in response to a behavior deemed wrong by an individual or group.

Punishments range from mild to harsh, but they are always about doing something negative or even painful to the child in order to deter repeated misbehavior. Examples are spanking, grounding, taking away privileges, and time-outs. Punishments are an easy way to gain short-term compliance, but these methods can cause fear and resentment and damage to the relationship and fail to teach the child what is right.

Here are 10 teaching alternatives to punishments.

1. *Time-in.* When children show signs of emotional dysregulation, they need the help of caring adults to help them calm themselves. Time-in differs from time-outs in that the child is brought into your lap or in close proximity of you. You should interact with the child during this time, including hugs, eye-to-eye contact,

and conversation. During the time-in, help to calm the child down, and then discuss what happened. An example may be, "You wanted your brother's toy, so you hit him. Hitting is not okay. I'll help you learn a better way." Give your child alternatives to hitting, such as clapping, squeezing a stress ball, or using one of the calm down tools I'll discuss in this section. When your child is calm and understands the limit, time-in is over.

2. *Calm-Down Spot.* This should be a relaxing, calming area where you can go with your child, or your child can go alone if she prefers, and should be personally designed for your child with soft blankets, books, and emotional regulation tools which are discussed next. You can model for your child how to use this by going to the calm down spot when you get upset. It should be an inviting area where your child wants to go and should never be used in a punitive manner.

3. *Emotional regulation.* There are many tools that you can offer your child to use to help regulate him when he gets into a state of dysregulation or upset. When children are upset, they are incapable of rational thought. When children are calm, they take in what we teach them. The key is to get them calm and regulated before we offer correction. There are many, many ways to help your child to emotional regulation and it will

really be trial and error to figure out what works best for your child. Some like physical activities, such as clapping or tug of war. Others prefer tactile activities such as shredding paper. Some find release in popping balloons. Stress ball balloons work well for many kids. (Fill balloons with playdough or small beads. Put one balloon inside another to prevent spills.)

Calm down jars made of water, food coloring, glitter, and glitter glue, also called mind jars, may also work for your child to bring her to a state of calm.

4. *Problem-solving.* Instead of imposing a consequence on your child for a specific behavior, have her be involved in the process of resolution and/or making amends by working through the problem with her and having her (or helping her) come up with a solution.

5. *Natural consequences.* We don't always need to step in. Life is great teacher and sometimes our best option is to sit back and let the natural consequences of our children's choices take effect. Of course, you have to be discretionary about what you will allow here and take age and maturity into consideration. I wouldn't let my 2-year-old freeze without a coat because he refused to wear one, but if my child was 9 and refused to wear a

coat, I would allow him to experience the consequence of getting cold.

6. *Logical consequences.* Ideally, all consequences should come as a result of problem-solving. For instance, your child may decide to do chores to earn back the money to replace something broken. The chores are the consequence for his action, but they were his idea or mutually decided upon and do not feel punitive. However, there may be times when you need to deliver a logical consequence. For young children, taking away the toy that just got thrown is a logical consequence for that action. For older children, it may be turning off the TV until homework gets done (if she won't stop watching it long enough to do her homework). Logical consequences should always be given with kindness and empathy, showing that your *intent* is to teach, not to punish.

7. *Ignore.* Think in terms of biggies and smallies. Dr. Sears discusses this in *The Discipline Book.*[12] Divide your child's behaviors into biggies (hurting self, others, or property) which need your attention, and smallies (nuisances and annoyances) which are not worth you getting upset over. These childish irresponsibilities will self-correct with time and maturity. Harmless behaviors fade both as your tolerance level widens and

as you avoid reactions that reinforce the behavior.

8. *Set up the environment for success.* It is impossible to control your child, but you can control his environment and help set him up for success. Put breakable things out of reach. Make his play area child-friendly where he is free to explore as he wishes. If he is a climber, stack cushions for him to climb over and he won't be heading for the kitchen counter. Controlling the environment will give your children more freedom and you more peace as you won't have to be redirecting him away from something potentially dangerous every few minutes.

9. *Redirection.* This works well with crawlers and toddlers. If your 1 year old is heading for the hot stove, a smack or punishment isn't necessary to teach her that it is hot. Hold her up near the stove at a safe distance and allow her to feel the heat radiating from it. Tell her it is hot and will hurt. Then remove her from the area and get her interested in another activity. If she is persistent in going back to the stove, you may need to place a gate up at the kitchen, but if you get her involved in something interesting enough, the stove will lose its appeal. It is our responsibility to control the environment, not theirs to know what is dangerous or not dangerous at this young age.

10. *Humor.* Sometimes we take ourselves way too seriously. I promise it is okay to break out of that serious role and just have fun and be silly. Laughter helps you connect with your kids and it's good for your health! Laughter strengthens relationships, attracts others to us, enhances teamwork, helps defuse conflict, and promotes group bonding. Humor and playful communication triggers positive feelings and fosters emotional connection. When we laugh with one another a positive bond is created. This bond acts as a strong buffer against stress, disagreements, and disappointments. Not only does laughter bond us when we're feeling good, but it protects us in times of adversity.

17

Twenty-One Days

"Your present circumstances don't determine where you can go; they merely determine where you start." - Nido Qubein[13]

It doesn't matter if you have a newborn or a teenager, you can begin where you are right now with positive parenting. There are no tricks, no formulas, no rules to implement; there is only connection. Children are amazingly forgiving and accepting people, especially when they see our sincerity and willingness to change.

If you're changing course from punitive parenting, a family meeting is a good place to start to explain your new decision and discuss what it means for the family. Be open and honest with your children, admit past mistakes, ask for forgiveness, and lay out what is going to change. Do not think you will lose credential by being real. When children see us admitting our mistakes and changing course, it teaches them that they can do the same, and that's handy knowledge to have as they head into adolescence and adulthood.

Start your new journey by focusing primarily on

connection. If your children are having a lot of behavioral problems right now, let the "smallies" go and only correct the "biggies" while you build your connection. Listen openly and intently to your children as they share their feelings and ideas. Play with them daily, and focus your attention on them entirely during play. Find ways to laugh together. Get interested in what they're interested in. Use nurturing touch – hugs, back rubs, massage – whatever your child enjoys. These are all ways to build connection. As your connection grows, behavioral problems will shrink.

When you have to correct a "biggie," do so with teaching in mind. Don't attack or condemn and remember to be respectful in your words and actions. Restore and repair afterward. Use problem-solving as much as possible to teach your child how to correct her own mistakes and keep her own behavior in line. The more self-discipline she has, the less you have to correct.

If your children are older, expect that they may test you a bit to see if this is for real. This is a normal response. Be consistent and they will adapt. Envision yourself as a steady oak tree, firmly rooted and unshakeable. Whatever storms come and go, you remain standing strong. You are steady enough to endure the heavy rain and whipping wind (the emotional storms of your child) without getting blown away yourself.

Journal Your Way to Success

It is said that it takes 21 days to create a habit. Whether this is your first introduction to positive parenting or you've been practicing it for a while, we are all works in progress with room for growth and improvement.

I invite you to take the next 21 days to commit to being a more positive parent. Start a journal to keep track of goals, progress, and accomplishments. The following are 21 prompts to fill each day of this challenge.

Day one: What is the relationship with your child like at this moment? How can it be improved?

Day two: Where do you need to grow or improve?

Day three: What part of the day causes the most stress and how can it be changed?

Day four: Are your expectations too high? Too low? Age appropriate?

Day five: Write 5 good qualities for each child.

Day six: How can you put a spotlight on your child's good qualities?

Day seven: Are you *that one person* for your child? Do you see their light and reflect it back? Who is your *one person*?

Day eight: What habits do you have that you don't want your child to pick up? What is the plan for dropping those habits?

Day nine: Write a favorite memory that you have of your child. Go back to that time, recall how you felt. Feel it again.

Day ten: The most important thing you can do today for your child is _____.

Day eleven: Write down what inspires you to be a better parent and person.

Day twelve: Your ultimate parenting goal is _____.

Day thirteen: Which behaviors trigger you the most?

Day fourteen: What can you do when you get triggered to avoid blowing up? Write down an anger action plan.

Day fifteen: What is wonderful about this parenting season that you are currently in? What are you really enjoying about this time?

Day sixteen: What will you miss the most when this season is over?

Day seventeen: Is your agenda too full? Are you stretched too thin? What can you let go of?

Day eighteen: Are your thoughts mostly negative or mostly positive? Write down 3 positive thoughts you want to keep circling in your mind.

Day nineteen: Is there one regret that you're holding on to? Can you forgive yourself and let it go? Wouldn't you want your child to do the same?

Day twenty: What wishes or prayers do you have for your children?

Day twenty-one: What do you want your legacy to be?

Also write the answer these questions each evening in your journal:

Was I present today?
How well did I handle my emotions?
Did I connect with my child?
Did we play?
What can I improve on tomorrow?

This kind of guided journaling will focus your attention daily on your goals. Along with the prompts and end questions, track your progress in your journal and any noticeable differences in your children and the atmosphere of your home. Be sure to celebrate your successes and give yourself credit for making this important change in yourself and your family.

18

You're Changing the World

"One generation full of deeply loving parents would change the brain of the next generation, and with that, the world." - Charles Raison[14]

Dr. Gordon Neufeld, author of *Hold On To Your Kids*[15], has said, "Children must never work for our love; they must rest in it. We have gone to a practice of parenting and teaching that makes them work for the contact and closeness - that puts them in charge of the relationship. We make them work at keeping us close. We might get more compliance, but we get a deeply restless child, and we're giving rise to a whole generation of children who are restless to the core. Our yearning as parents...should be to give them rest."

When we provide our children with rest, when they know that our love is not dependent upon their behavior but is always constant and concrete, we allow them to rest in our love. Dr. Neufeld states that "all growth emanates from a place of rest."

As you practice positive parenting and unconditional love in your home, you are giving that rest to your child. The positive impact of parenting from a connected relationship will not only permeate your home but will trickle out into all of your child's relationships.

Imagine for a moment a generation of human beings who were raised in a state of emotional rest. The potential of such a generation is astounding.

We have an amazing opportunity, parents. We are raising the future of humanity, and love is the key to heal us all. It's time we strip away all of the "knowledge" that has been forced on us through culture, media, and community and get back, quite literally, to the heart of parenting. We were made for love and connection, and so it only makes sense to approach raising these human beings from a strong foundation of these basic and primal needs.

The relationships we build with our children last a lifetime. Ultimately, love is the only leverage we have with our kids. Fear-based parenting only works as long as it can be physically or emotionally enforced, but love is a more effective motivator over time. Through being kind and firm, consistent and empathetic, we allow our children optimal development. When the child-rearing is done, the loving bond you have built is what will make your relationship with your adult child fruitful and enjoyable. Positive parenting keeps that relationship intact while teaching and guiding your child to his or her fullest potential.

I want to personally commend you for making the effort to the best parent you can be. Thank you for raising a connected child. Marianne Williamson says, "There is no single effort more radical in it's potential for saving the world than a transformation in the way we raise our children."[16]

Because you have chosen a transformation, you are part of this movement to send forth connected and emotionally healthy people, and the fruits of your labor will be seen for generations to come. You matter. You're making a difference.

May you be blessed.

Works Cited

1. Jeanne, S., J. Jaelline, and J. Jaelline. N.p.. Web. 1 Jul 2013. <http://www.helpguide.org/mental/eqa_attachment_bond.htm>.

2. White, Chris. N.p.. Web. 1 Jul 2013. <http://www.pbs.org/thisemotionallife/blogs/attachment-and-development-resilience>.

3. Markham, Laura. N.p.. Web. 1 Jul 2013. <http://www.ahaparenting.com/parenting-tools/raise-great-kids/emotionally-intelligent-child/emotional-intelligence>.

4. Waxler, Jerry. "Anger, Aggression, and Fight or Flight." *Mental Health Survival Guide*. N.p.. Web. 1 Jul 2013. <http://www.mental-health-survival-guide.com/brochures/anger.html>.

5. Petersen, Andrea. "Study Says Yelling Is As Hurtful as Hitting." *The Wallstreet Journal*. (2013): n. page. Web. 18 Jan. 2015. <http://www.wsj.com/articles/SB10001424127887323623304579055302147114522>.

6. Hamilton, Jon. "Scientists Say Child's Play Helps Build A Better Brain." *npr.org*. N.p., 06 08 2014. Web. 17 Jan. 2015.

<http://www.npr.org/blogs/ed/2014/08/06/3363612 77/scientists-say-childs-play-helps-build-a-better-brain>.

7. Ferrer, M., and A. Fugate. n. page. <http://edis.ifas.ufl.edu/fy570>.

8. *Proverbs. The Holy Bible ESV: English Standard Version: Containing the Old and New Testaments.* Wheaton, IL: Crossway Bibles, 2007. Print.

9. Cloud, H. *Changes that heal: How to understand your past to ensure a healthier future.* Grand Rapids, MI: Zondervan, 1992. Print.

10. N.p.. Web. 1 Jul 2013. <http://www.searchquotes.com/quotation/Power_is_ of_two_kinds._One_is_obtained_by_the_fear_of_pu nishment_and_the_other_by_acts_of_love._Powe/67 9/>.

11. Adapted from: Bailey, B. A. *Easy to love, difficult to discipline.* New York, NY: William Morrow and Company, Inc., 2000. Print.

12. Sears, William, and Martha Sears. *The Discipline Book.* NYC: Little, Brown and Co., 1995. Print.

13. N.p.. Web. 1 Jul 2013. <http://www.brainyquote.com/quotes/quotes/n/nido qubein178331.html>.

14. Vignando, Yvette. N.p.. Web. 1 Jul 2013.

<http://www.happychild.com.au/articles/how-supportive-parenting-impacts-your-childs-brain>.

15. Neufeld, Gordon. *Hold on to your kids: why parents need to matter more than peers*. New Your: Ballantine Books Trade Paperback Edition, 2004. Print.

16. Williamson, Marianne. "There is no single effort more radical in its potential for saving the world than a transformation in the way we raise our chilren." . N.p., Online Posting to *Goodreads*. Web. 22 Jan. 2015. <https://www.goodreads.com/quotes/350499-there-is-no-single-effort-more-radical-in-its-potential>.

Appendix A
Popular Blog Posts

Ten Things That Are More Important Than Discipline

Parenting is a very complex task. If we're not careful, we will become too focused on one aspect and let the others fall by the wayside. Many times, I see parents who are intently focused on discipline, in the more traditional sense of modifying behavior by external motivators. Sometimes we get very caught up in *what do I do when...* or *how do I get my kid to...* and we lose sight of the bigger picture.

The truth is that there are many things that are more important in shaping our children than the methods and techniques we use to modify their behavior.

Here are 10 things that are more important than any method you choose, in no particular order.

1. *Relationship.* The connection that we have with our children greatly impacts how they accept our guidance. Our relationship sets an example for how

relationships should be throughout the rest of their lives. If we have a healthy relationship based on respect, empathy, and compassion, we have set a standard. They will grow to expect that this is what a relationship looks like and will likely not settle for less. If, however, our relationship is based on control, coercion, and manipulation, well, you see where I'm going with this.

Children are more likely to listen to and cooperate with an adult whom they are connected to. In other words, if we build trust and open communication when they are small, they will come to us when they are not so small. Our attachment helps wire healthy brains, and our responses set the tone for how they respond to us.

2. *Your lens.* When you look at your child, who do you see? Do you see the positives or the negatives? The way you think about him influences the way you treat him. Your thoughts also influence the way you feel emotionally and physically throughout the day. "He is in the terrible twos" will cause you to look for terrible things, to focus on them, and therefore try to correct them...constantly.

Try to turn negative thoughts like this into positive thoughts like, "He is inquisitive." Try to start seeing behavior as a clue that calls for help rather than something that needs squashed immediately. Correction is not needed nearly as often as you might think.

3. *Your relationship with your significant other.* Your kids are watching and learning. The way you and your partner treat each other again sets a standard. Happy parents make happy kids. The foundation of a happy family is a strong, loving relationship between the two of you. Do everything in your power to have the best possible relationship with your spouse or other parent. If they see the two of you getting along and supporting each other, they will mirror you and will likely get along with each other and their friends. Every single ounce of energy that you put into your relationship will come back to you tenfold through your children.

4. *The atmosphere of your home.* All of the things mentioned above come together to create the atmosphere in your home. If you have loving and connected relationships, you likely have a warm atmosphere in your home. If there is discord between you and your spouse, or you and your child, or your child and your other child, then the overall atmosphere will suffer. Have you ever gone to someone's home and could just feel a negative atmosphere? You want your

home to be a haven, a safe, warm, inviting, and loving place for all family members.

5. *How you relate to others.* How do you treat the bank teller, the store clerk, the telemarketer? What about your parents and your in-laws? They are watching your example.

6. *Community.* Are you involved in your community? Aside from setting an example, there are valuable lessons to be learned from volunteering, supporting a local cause, attending church, or donating items. Seeing a bigger picture, how their acts can influence many lives, will give them a sense of responsibility and reinforce good values.

7. *School.* Whether you choose private school, public school, homeschooling, or unschooling, your choice will have an impact on your child; choose with care. *Peers have a big influence on children, but if our relationship is where it should be, our influence will still be stronger.*

8. *Your cup.* If your cup is empty, you won't be able to give your child what he really needs or what you really want to give. Don't try to fit in self-care after everybody else is taken care of. You have to take care of you so you

can take care of them. If your cup is full, you are more patient, more empathetic, and have more energy. Not only that, but *a child who sees his parents respect themselves learns to have self-respect.* Put yourself back on your list.

9. *Media.* Television. Video games. Social media. They are always sending messages to your kids. Be aware of what your kids are getting from what they're watching. Talk about what they see in the media. These often provide good opportunities to talk about situations we wouldn't otherwise encounter.

10. *Basic needs.* Adequate nutrition, sleep, and exercise are not only essential for the well-being of your child but also influence behavior. According to Maslow's hierarchy of needs (McLeod), people are not motivated to fulfill "higher" needs such as socialization or self-actualization until more basic needs, including safety, are met. Not making sure these needs are met unnecessarily holds back your child from reaching his full potential.

Reference: McLeod, Saul. "Maslow's Heirarchy of Needs." *Simply Psychology.* n. page. Web. 22 Jan. 2015. <http://www.simplypsychology.org/maslow.html>.

Healthy Responses to Children's Emotions

In an article titled Five Healthy Responses to a Child's Natural Emotions, Liz Hale outlined the findings from a research study at the University of Washington which was done under the direction of Dr. John Gottman. (Hale) I would like to elaborate on the 5 healthy responses mentioned in the article, which are:

Recognize the emotion.
Increase intimacy with emotion.
Listen for and validate emotion.
Label emotion.
Set limits with emotion.

How do you put this into practice? Let's go through a couple of scenarios.

Scenario One: Your 2 year old daughter is having a tantrum in the store because you won't buy her a specific toy. She is so upset, she begins to throw things out of your cart.

1. Recognize the emotion. What is your daughter feeling at this moment? Anger. Frustration.

Disappointment. Just take a moment to breathe and put yourself in her little shoes.

2. Increase intimacy with emotion. Empathize with what your child is feeling. No feeling is ever bad, wrong, or unacceptable. When you empathize, you can use this as a moment to connect with your child on a deep level. "I know it can be upsetting to not get what you want."

3. Listen for and validate the emotion. "I understand that you're upset. I see how upset you are. You really want that toy."

4. Label emotion. "You're angry that I can't buy you that toy."

5. Set limits with emotion. "I understand that you feel angry. I will help you with those feelings, but I can't let you throw things." If you need to remove her from the cart and sit on a bench with her for a few minutes (or on the floor), do so. Don't worry about who's watching. You're teaching your child emotional intelligence!

This lets your child know that her feelings matter, that you understand her, that you accept her, bad feelings and all, and also sets the limit on how to act out her feelings.

This isn't mentioned in the article, but I will add that it's a good idea to carry a little calm down jar or I Spy jar in your purse, or a tablet and pencil for drawing out feelings, whatever helps your child to calm down, and a stress ball. It's not really about distracting them away from the emotion but rather about validating the emotion and helping them return to balance. I love the stress balls in the link. She can pick out her feeling from the faces on the balls, and then "squeeze her mad out" instead of throwing things out of your cart.

Scenario Two: Your 12 year old son found out that his "best friend" was talking about him behind his back. He had a big fight with his friend. He's visibly upset about the incident.

1. Recognize the emotion. What is your son feeling? Betrayed. Sad. Angry. Hurt.

2. Increase intimacy with emotion. Empathize with him. Pre-teen squabbles seem like small stuff in our adult world filled with "real" problems, but this is a big deal to him. Acknowledge that.

3. Listen for and validate the emotion. Talk to him. At

12, you don't have to guess. He can tell you how the incident made him feel. "I hear that your friend really hurt your feelings."

4. Label emotion. "You're angry that he betrayed you like that, and sad that you feel like you've lost your friend."

5. Set limits with emotion. In this case, unless he's threatening retaliation or doing something inappropriate, there is no need to set a limit.

Number 5 would have been better stated "set limits with acting out emotion." You can't set a limit on an emotion, it is what it is, all you can do is teach him how to get through his emotions. Of course, if he's threatening to start a rumor on his friend, or punch him in the face, you'll have to set a limit and help him brainstorm better ways to deal. "I know you feel like punching him for hurting you like that. What would happen if you punched him? Violence is never the answer. What might you do to make things right? What would make you feel better?"

"In the last decade or so, science has discovered a tremendous amount about the role emotions play in our lives. Researchers have found that even more than

IQ, your emotional awareness and abilities to handle feelings will determine your success and happiness in all walks of life, including family relationships." - John Gottman (Anton)

References:

1. (Hale) Hale, Liz. "5 healthy responses to a child's natural emotions." KSL.com. 27 09 2011: n. page. Print. <http://www.ksl.com/index.php?nid=148&sid=17427075>.

2. (Anton) Anton, Richard. "Emotional Intelligence." Anton Counseling and Health Psychology. N.p., n. d. Web. 22 Jan. 2015. <http://www.antonpsych.org/site/emotional_intelligence>.

Ignoring Their Cries

I am, at times, taken aback by the practices we, culturally, will accept and perform without question. A friend recently asked for advice on her Facebook page because she said her child's (a preschooler) reaction to anything was to cry. As I set there reading her friends' recommendations, my heart sank. Most all of them told her to ignore him when he cries. Some said to punish him or send him away, and my thought was my goodness, where is the empathy?

Empathy is lacking in American culture all over the board, but a severe lack of empathy in dealing with children's emotions is disturbingly prevalent. We are given the advice to ignore them almost as soon as they come out of the womb in a sad and misguided attempt to "train" them, from allowing them to helplessly cry in their crib so that they learn to "self-soothe," to ignoring the screams of a distressed toddler so she doesn't "continue throwing fits for attention," to ignoring the cries of preschoolers and older children so as not to spoil them, and, for boys, feminize them. (Yes, sadly that is still a problem).

Our friends tell us they do it. The internet tells us it is

okay. Some parenting experts advise it. Perhaps even your pediatrician may recommend it. However, the fact that everyone else is doing it doesn't make it right, neither does the fact that it is socially acceptable. I could bore you with study after study of the negative effects on children's brains and emotional development when they are ignored, left to cry alone without the comfort a parent's loving arms, but for goodness' sake, I shouldn't have to. Where is our moral compass?

How did we come to accept and believe it is okay to ignore our children when they are upset? Is it the lack of empathy shown to us when we were children that makes it so easy for us to be apathetic to it?

It seems we have come to the conclusion that there are only 2 options. Give in to their cries, thereby spoiling them and turning them into dreadful brats, or ignoring them to keep that from happening.

But there is a wonderful third option! One that doesn't give in to the child or isolate him.

EMPATHY.

It doesn't come easily to many of us, especially if we were deprived of it as children ourselves, but it can, and should be, learned and passed down generation to generation. I will not, for the sake of post length, get into allowing infants to cry-it-out as I will certainly go off on a tangent, but for toddlers, preschoolers, and the older child, it looks something like this.

Your toddler is tired and cranky. The slightest thing sends him over the edge into a huge crying fit. I can tell you with certainty that he is not breaking down for his benefit. He is not manipulating you or trying to make your life difficult. He is overwhelmed, and giving him comfort will no more make him want to have more meltdowns than your friend giving you a shoulder to lean on will make you want to have to lean on her more. Don't withhold affection or attention during his time of distress. He needs you.

If your preschooler wants a cookie for breakfast, and you deny her the cookie causing her to cry, there is no need to ignore her OR give her the cookie. The third option allows you to say, "I see that you are upset over the cookie. You really want it, but that isn't a healthy breakfast, and I want you to be healthy." Understand her view. Validate her feelings. She is a human being. If your older child pouts or cries because you won't buy him a new video game, sending him to his room isn't going to resolve his feelings, but only cause more negative feelings to build. You know what it is like to want things and not be able to get them. You probably experience that feeling every payday! I do! Empathize. "You're upset about the video game. I know what that feels like. I'm sorry you're feeling this way. I just cannot get it right now." Sure, it may require a whole lot more patience from you than sending him away or blocking him out, but remember...

"You're not managing an inconvenience, you're raising a human being." - Kittie Frantz

Reference:
Frantz, Kittie. ""Remember, you are not managing an inconvenience; You are raising a human being." ." . N.p., Web. 22 Jan. 2015. <http://www.goodreads.com/quotes/226587-remember-you-are-not-managing-an-inconvenience-you-are-raising>.

How to Respect Your Child Through Challenging Behavior

Respecting our children is the heart of positive parenting, but how do you maintain that respect through challenging behavior?

I received an email from a sweet mom asking how to deal with her child's sudden upset at baths. Her toddler developed a sudden aversion to bath time and would cry and fight to not get in the bath. Her husband wanted to force baths anyway, and it ended up being a huge power struggle in her home.

Some might agree with the dad in this situation, saying that "giving in" would just let the child feel she was in charge. On the contrary, empathizing with your child's upset, however offbeat it may seem to you, shows her that she is important and that her feelings are acceptable and understood. It's respectful to her and important for your relationship that you truly look at baths from her point of view and understand that she has big feelings about it. However, she needs to be cleaned. I would suggest trying a few options. Perhaps she'd prefer a shower, or just being wiped off while standing in the tub, or even beside the tub. As long as she gets clean, mission accomplished. I assure you it won't give her the impression that she rules the roost, nor will it mean she will never bath again. Maybe she's afraid she'll go down the drain. Maybe she got water in her eyes last time and it stung. Try to understand her fear, find out where it came from, and help her work through that. Eventually, this will pass. In the meantime, she'll know that her feelings are important.

Our culture is so caught up in control. Parents have to be in control! We're in charge! We're so afraid of raising the kind of child that our culture so openly disdains. Spoiled. Bratty. Disrespectful. Frankly, we're more worried about our own shame we'd face than about what our kids are feeling. We are a culture terrified of permissiveness. Alfie Kohn says, "The dominant problem with parenting in our society isn't permissiveness, but the fear of permissiveness. We're so worried about spoiling kids that we often end up over controlling them." (Kohn)

I agree with Alfie. I certainly don't see much "permissiveness" where I live. Quite the contrary, in fact. However, when ditching the old paradigm of control and fear, it can be easy to fall into permissiveness, but don't be mistaken - positive parenting is not about a lack of limits. It's not about not disciplining children. It's not about respecting them to the extreme degree that we never tell them "no." That isn't healthy for the child either.

Alfie also says this, "The most popular false dichotomy in parenting runs as follows: "We need to take a hard line with kids and stop letting them do anything they feel like." In effect, traditional discipline is contrasted with permissiveness. Either I punish my child or else I let her "get away with" whatever she did. Either I take a hard line or I draw no line at all." (Kohn)

How often do I hear this? If we don't draw a hard line, people think we draw no lines at all, and that is simply not true. If there is one thing that I wish people would understand about positive parenting is that, as a whole, we are not permissive parents! Sure, there are a few in the bunch, but they don't represent what we stand for as a whole.

But I digress. Back to the original question here. How do you respect your child without being a pushover? You empathize and stick to your limits. Respecting your child doesn't mean she always gets her way. That would, at times, be disrespectful to her if what she wants is dangerous or unhealthy! Rather, it means you take her feelings, her personhood, into regard when you interact with her. When you have to say no, you don't have to draw a hard line. You don't have to shout her down in order to assert yourself. Respect, by definition, means this: A feeling of deep admiration for someone or something elicited by their abilities, qualities, or achievements. Even when you have to set your foot down, remember your deep admiration for her. When you have to say "no" to more candy or "can I stay up later pleeeease," or to that party he was invited to, remember your deep admiration; remember your love, and then come to him with your assertion, with your "no" from that place of love. "I understand that you really want more candy, but too much is not healthy. Would you like an apple instead?"

"I realize all your friends will be at that party. You must feel very disappointed that you cannot go."

Will they automatically accept your limit because you were nice about it? Maybe or maybe not. They may very well still be very upset with you, and that's okay. Be respectful in your interactions, even if they're not. They're watching your example.

The message I want to convey is that parenting has so little to do with punishments and so much to do with relationships. How well we attach and bond, how well we set boundaries, how well we listen, how well we love, that is what shapes us! For generations, parents have shaped "fine" but deeply restless human beings. We may know "how to act" but we're losing sight of how to love, how to bond, how to have healthy relationships. This is evident in our broken homes, the rise in depression and mental illness, suicide rates, and so forth. We have to teach them more than just "how to act." We have to teach them how to love, how to bond, how to deal with their emotions, how to have healthy relationships, and how to get out of relationships that aren't healthy. Our relationship with them is the one they will come to base all relationships on, so let's not base it on control and fear.

"People grow close not through monitoring one another's behavior but by working together, talking together, celebrating together, weeping together. Relationships develop when people are there for each other - and that's as true for parents and children as it is for anyone else."- Sally Clarkson, The Mission of Motherhood (Clarkson

References:

1. (Kohn) Kohn, Alfie. ""The dominant problem with parenting in our society isn't permissiveness, but the

fear of permissiveness. We're so worried about spoiling kids that we often end up over controlling them." ." . N.p., Web. 22 Jan. 2015. <http://www.goodreads.com/work/quotes/1390192-unconditional-parenting-moving-from-rewards-and-punishments-to-love-and>.

2. (Kohn) Kohn, Alfie. "Rethinking Baumrind's "Authoritative" Parenting." *Alfie Kohn*. N.p., n. d. Web. 22 Jan. 2015. <http://www.alfiekohn.org/rethinking-baumrinds-authoritative-parenting/>.

3. (Clarkson) Clarkson, Sally. *The Mission of Motherhood*. Print.

Consequences that Teach

There is a disturbing new parenting trend for "creative consequences." But is shaming children really the way to go? Is it effective?

Brené Brown, PhD, LMSW has spent the last 12 years researching shame, guilt, and vulnerability. She states: "Shame, blame, disrespect, betrayal, and the withholding of affection damage the roots from which love grows," and very importantly, "Shame corrodes the very part of us that believes we are capable of change." (Brown)

That's big. That should cause us to stop and think.

Giving consequences with the intention of shaming, hurting, or humiliating a child is damaging. Sure, they may "work," but at what cost?

The purposes of consequences, however, should not be to make us famous or earn us a pat on the back from other parents, but to teach the child in a constructive way.

Shame and humiliation create fear, and research

indicates that the brain operates differently under fear. Under this threat, the brain reacts with increased blood flow to the survival centers of the brain and decreased blood flow to the higher thought centers. When the brain goes into this "survival mode," it becomes less capable of planning, receiving information, classifying data, and problem solving.

Guide to Giving Consquences That Teach

1. Give consequences with the intention of teaching, not the intention of punishing or making the child feel bad. Intention is important because the intention you have in your mind will influence the language and tone you use when you deliver the consequence. Be sure to be empathetic when delivering the consequence. Empathy calms the brain, removes the threat, and allows a person to take responsibility for this own behavior.

2. Let natural consequences happen where appropriate. Often we try to either rescue our child from the natural consequences of their actions OR we compound it by adding additional punishments on top of it. Let's say your child left her toy in the driveway and it got ran over. Rescuing would be buying her a new toy immediately. Adding additional punishment would be

grounding her for leaving it outside. The natural consequence, however, is simply that now her toy is broken. If she wants to replace it, she can earn the money to do so by doing extra chores.

3. Imposed consequences should be related to the offense. If your child hits his brother, then taking away his iPad for a period of time doesn't teach what he should do when he hurts his brother. A related (or logical) consequence would be to have him problem solve a way to repair the relationship with his brother (write him a note, make him a card, etc) and to talk about ways of handling his frustration or anger so that he has tools besides hitting (deep breaths, walking away, clapping, hitting a pillow).

4. Problem-solving is a great way to teach children how to be accountable and responsible. The more involved they are in the process, the more they learn. Most times, problem-solving is the best way to go. Teach your child the process of righting wrongs and repairing rifts in relationships. These skills will serve your child all of his life.

5. Don't bring it up. After the consequence has been given or the problem has been solved, it's over. Don't rehash the incident, but get on with a pleasant day.

6. Connect. Make sure your child knows it was her

behavior you didn't approve of, not HER. Find ways to reconnect. This models for your child what you were just teaching; how to repair relationships.

Ultimately, our goal is to raise responsible children. Teaching through natural or logical consequences or problem-solving isn't going to get you any media coverage, but it will get you a responsible child who doesn't resent you for years to come.

Reference:
(Brown) Brown, Brene. "Shame, blame, disrespect, betrayal, and the withholding of affection damage the roots from which love grows. Love can only survive these injuries if they are acknowledged, healed and rare." . N.p., E-mail.
<https://www.goodreads.com/author/quotes/162578.Bre n_Brown>.

Dangling Love

Picture this:

Sara has been very busy with the children today. She has played in the floor with her toddler, laughing, making memories. They made a car out of a cardboard box in between nursing and caring for her infant as well. The children are well taken care of and happy, but the house...

The mess from the day's play is lying around when her husband, John, gets home. John shoots her a look of disapproval that makes her heart sink. Hasn't she been good enough, today? She goes over to connect with a hug, and he withdrawals from her. Feeling the sting of rejection, she immediately starts picking up the mess. John goes to take a shower. When he gets out, the mess is picked up, and the house looks good. He nods and gives his wife a loving hug. "This looks much better. Thank you."

What sort of feelings did this story bring up for you? How did it leave you feeling about John? About Sara? What can you deduce about their relationship from this story?

The question was posed on my Facebook page recently, "If he doesn't pick up his toys, should I give him a hug as a reward?!"

Friends, love is not a reward. Hugs, attention, affection, kind words - these are not rewards to be dangled in front of a child, only given when he performs to our liking. These are a child's lifeline. They should be given without condition, without hesitation. Always.

We've developed this rather strange idea that loving children too much is bad for them, but if we offer just enough love at the right times, they will jump through hoops to get it. And they probably will, but they shouldn't have to. Withholding love and affection most certainly works to control a child because this is very real need, and they must get it met in whatever way they can, but take a moment to stop and feel the sadness that the child feels - the rejection, the feeling of needing to get it right before being worthy of love and affection.

I imagine Sara feeling a sense of relief, and even loved, once John gave her his affection and approval. I also imagine there is emotional instability and pain.

Please don't make children earn your affection. As Dr.

Gordon Neufeld said, "If children want attention, then why on earth wouldn't we give it to them?" (Neufeld)

Too much love won't spoil. Kindness doesn't provoke poor behavior. Respect doesn't invite disrespect. This is backwards thinking which has caused us to feel trapped into being too harsh for too long. Generations of children are still searching and longing for unconditional love.

Let's make a change.

Reference:

(Neufeld) Neufeld, Gordon, perf. *Why Children Need Rest and How to Provide It*. YouTube, Web. 22 Jan 2015. <https://www.youtube.com/watch?v=nUHnMfa_aKE>.

Appendix B

365 Days of Play

Spring/Summer Outdoor Activities

1. Run through a sprinkler together.

2. Go on a hike.

3. Make a sidewalk chalk creation.

4. Jump on a trampoline.

5. Go on a bug hunt.

6. Fill a kiddie pool with water and add bubble bath.

7. Play baseball.

8. Hang water balloon pinatas from a tree, and hit them with a large stick.

9. Go bird watching.

10. Fill water bottles with colored water and spray paint the bubbles in the bubble pool.

11. Camp out in the back yard.

12. Take poster board and paint to the sidewalk and create art.

13. Fill water balloons with shaving cream and throw them at each other.

14. Go on a family bike ride.

15. Mix baking soda and water and freeze in a muffin tin. Use these ice blocks for cool summer play. Spray vinegar on the block creation and watch it fizz!

16. Go on a scavenger hunt.

17. Play in a sand box.

18. Paint sand castles with food coloring.

19. Set up an outdoor obstacle course.

20. Pick a bouquet of fresh wild flowers.

21. Freeze small toys in a large pan of water until solid. Use a rubber mallet to break them free.

22. If the pool has a slide, lather it up with shaving cream for a fun sensory experience.

23. Make sidewalk chalk paint. (Recipe in Appendix C)

24. Make bubble snakes. Cut the end off a water bottle. Cover with a sock and tape it securely. Mix dish liquid and water, add food coloring. Dip the bottle in the bubble solution and blow into the bottle!

25. Make gigantic bubble solution and create amazingly big bubbles. (Recipe in Appendix C)

26. Fly kites.

27. Go fishing.

28. Hide small toys in a sand box. Go on a excavation!

29. Have a water balloon fight.

30. Play flashlight tag after dark.

31. Have a sack race.

32. Make mudpies.

33. Throw rocks in the creek. Learn to skip rocks.

34. Build an outdoor fort.

35. Make an backyard fairy garden. Use your imaginations!

36. Go on a picnic.

37. Plant and grow a small garden, or just one pot per child.

38. Play freeze tag.

39. On a clear night, gaze at the moon and stars. Telescope optional!

40. Play on a Slip 'N Slide.

41. Gather a bunch of stones and create a labrynth.

42. Paint rocks with watercolors.

43. Jump in puddles.

44. Play dodge ball.

45. Make a homemade slip and slide with painter's plastic and a water hose. For a messier experience, add shaving cream.

46. Go apple picking.

47. Catch and release frogs.

48. Take books outside and read at the park or under a shade.

49. Lie on the ground and look at the clouds. Name shapes you see.

50. Play with a jump rope.

51. Play with a water table. Don't have one? Just fill up a large plastic bin.

52. Play flag football.

53. Explore the back yard with a magnifying glass.

54. Catch fireflies.

55. Play hopscotch.

56. Make a birdfeeder and feed the birds.

57. Make a birdbath by stacking clay pots and hot glue a large plastic dish on top. Fill with water.

58. Hang an old sheet on a fence or clothesline and spray paint with bottles of 1/2 water and 1/2 tempera paint.

59. Play with hula hoops.

60. Make sand volcanoes. Build up a sand scupture, leave a hole in the top. Pour in red food coloring and 2 tbs of baking soda. Pour in 1/2 cup of vinegar and watch the volcano erupt.

61. Make an outdoor music station by hanging pots, pans, jugs, lids - anything you want! Grab different instruments to play music with (wooden sticks, metal spoons, etc) and make music.

62. Play soccer.

63. Play duck, duck, goose.

64. Make a worm farm.

65. Set up small targets and blast them with water

guns.

66. Have a three-legged race.

67. Play horseshoes.

68. Have a clothesline art show.

69. Play a game of ringer with marbles.

70. Draw sidewalk chalk people and use them as "paper dolls." Dress them up!

71. Play basketball.

72. Draw a bullseye with sidewalk chalk and throw wet sponges at the target.

73. Fill squirt guns with colored water and make squirt gun art.

74. Make pet rocks! And rock people! Make a whole rock village!

75. Dig in the dirt.

76. Paint trees.

77. Grab binoculars and watch the wildlife.

78. Make a treasure map and go on a treasure hunt.

79. Play badminton.

80. Go on a nature walk and collect items of interest.

81. Make art with nature. Use rocks, leaves, flowers, grass, acorns - anything!

82. Look for four leaf clovers.

83. Make giant bubbles with a giant bubble recipe. (See Appendix C)

84. Wade in a creek.

85. Play hide and seek.

86. Play mini golf.

87. Toss a frisbee back and forth.

88. Blow bubbles.

89. Make a bug hotel for your backyard insects.

90. Go on an evening walk and watch the sunset.

91. Roll down hills together.

92. Use a large piece of cardboard as a sled and slide down the hill. No snow needed!

93. Play "Poohsticks" over a bridge.

94. Paint fences, sheds, or the sidewalk with sponge brushes and plain water.

95. Play croquet.

96. Wash and spray off the windows for soapy fun.

97. Look for tadpoles.

98. Gather daisies and make a daisy chain.

99. Make a homemade kite.

100. Ride a scooter.

101. Make colored ice blocks to stack and build with.

102. Catch a meteor shower.

103. Make a terrarium.

104. Play tennis.

105. Bob for apples.

106. Put glow sticks inside balloons, draw ghost faces on them, and hide them outside at night. Go on a ghosthunting adventure!

107. Take silly outdoor photos.

108. Have a water hose fight.

109. Make a car wash for toy cars.

110. Make boats out of pool noodles to play with in the pool.

111. Go horseback riding.

112. Go watch a ballgame.

113. Make a pool noodle marble run. Cut the pool noodle in half long-ways.

114. Play volleyball.

115. Make sidewalk chalk paint. (See Appendix C)

116. Feed the ducks at a pond.

117. Play Tic Tac Toe with sidewalk chalk.

118. Climb a tree.

119. Get together with friends and play Red Rover.

120. Go swimming.

Fall/Winter Outdoor Activities

121. Visit a pumpkin patch.

122. Rake up a pile of leaves and jump in them.

123. Go on an autumn hike through the colored trees and collect leaves.

124. Make leaf art on the ground.

125. Paint or carve pumpkins outside.

126. Go through a corn maze.

127. Make a homemade corn pit. Fill a small baby pool with two 50-pound bags of corn from the local feed store.

128. Go on a hayride.

129. Go geocaching.

130. Have a pie eating contest.

131. Set up empty 2-liter soda bottles and go bowling with small round gourds or pumpkins.

132. Try roller skating.

133. Build a campfire and roast marshmallows or make s'mores.

134. Visit the zoo.

135. Go ziplining.

136. Visit an amusement park.

137. Have a Nerf gun war.

138. Play outdoor Twister colored paper plates.

139. Do the Coke and Mentos explosion for some fun outdoor science.

140. Play hide and seek at the park.

141. Visit a lake and rent a paddleboat.

142. Hike a local park hiking trail.

143. Go snow tubing.

144. When the temperature falls below 32 degrees, blow bubbles and watch them freeze.

145. Build a snowman.

146. Go sledding.

147. Paint the snow with squeeze or spray bottles of food coloring and water.

148. Freeze water balloons, add food coloring inside the balloon before filling with water, and then take outside, peel off the balloons, and you have pretty giant ice marbles.

149. Have a snowball fight.

150. Go skiing.

151. Build a snow fort.

152. Make snow angels.

153. Using pans from the kitchen, mold crystal fairy castles in the snow.

154. Make colored ice cubes and then hide them in the snow for a wintery scavenger hunt.

155. Have a snowball toss game! Make a target by drawing a circle in the snow and see who can get the most inside the circle.

156. Play pin the nose on the snowman. Blindfold the kids and give them carrots. Spin them around and see if they can get the nose where it goes!

157. Use your snow boots to make art in the snow by walking around in patterns.

158. Go ice skating.

159. Try snowboarding.

160. Catch snowflakes on your tongue.

161. Play hockey.

162. Try ice fishing.

163. Wach a parade.

164. Visit a petting farm.

165. Go snowshoeing.

166. Have a snowball relay race.

Indoor Activities

167. Play balloon tennis. Tape a paper plate to a paint stick for the tennis racket and use a balloon as the tennis ball.

168. Play Twister.

169. Crepe paper the doorways and hallways of your home and let the kids bust through.

170. Make a pillow and blanket fort.

171. Have a family movie night.

172. Put water balloons in the bath water.

173. Make slime and play with it. (See Appendix C)

171. Paint in the bathtub with shaving cream mixed with food coloring.

175. Act out a story, like We're Going on a Bear Hunt.

176. Sculpt with homemade salt clay. (See Appendix C)

177. Make dinosaur fossils with playdough and toy dinosaurs. Imprint and let dry.

178. Have a pillow case sack race.

179. Pretend play Santa's workshop.

180. Bake and decorate cookies.

181. Make a bird feeder.

182. Go on a bedtime pretend adventure. Pretend to be flying to the moon or visit unknown lands.

183. Have a dance party.

184. Play traditional birthday party games even if it's nobody's birthday, like pin the tail on the donkey or bust a pinata.

185. Work on a scrapbook together.

186. Do karaoke.

187. Pretend play doctor's office.

188. Give the kids a big cardboard box and see what it becomes.

189. Create something out of crafty clay. (See Appendix C)

190. Play red light, green light.

191. Do a paper plate craft.

192. Play video games together.

193. Pretend play market.

194. Make paper airplanes and fly them.

195. Set up targets and get out the Nerf weapons.

196. Make a thumbprint craft.

197. Cuddle up under a blanket and read books.

198. Make sock puppets and put on a play.

199. Make oobleck. (See Appendix C)

200. Blow up balloons with glow sticks insdie and hang them from the bedroom ceiling for a delightful nightlight.

201. Let your kids help you plan and cook dinner.

202. Make and decorate a cake.

203. Pretend play airlines.

204. Make homemade ice cream.

205. Play simon says.

206. Play a classic board game.

207. Play musical chairs.

208. Make a time capsule to open next year.

209. Make salt dough ornaments. (See Appendix C)

210. Have an indoor picnic.

211. Play indoor hopscotch with masking tape on the floor.

212. Make a craft with popsicle sticks.

213. Make a band and put on a show.

214. Play hot potato.

215. Pretend play veterinarian.

216. Make a paperchain.

217. Create snacklaces. Thread cheerios, Froot Loops, or pretzels on yarn or string.

218. Play with water beads.

219. Make homemade Moon Sand. (See Appendix C)

220. Make a sensory tub for your child to explore. There are a lot of ideas online.

221. Make shadow puppets on the wall.

222. Have an indoor snowball fight with balled up socks.

223. Play ring around the rosie.

224. Make Rice Krispies treates.

225. Pretend play knights and dragons.

226. Set up a science lab with beakers, test tubes, water, color tablets, and measuring spoons.

227. Build with wooden blocks.

228. Paint with scratch and sniff watercolors. (See Appendix C)

229. Set aside one hour for superheroes or tea party or whatever your child chooses.

230. Have a themed day like wear your clothes inside out or wear something silly.

231. Pretend play dentist.

232. Play hide and seek inside.

233. Make an indoor obstacle course.

234. Pretend play animals.

235. Use empty water bottles and a ball and go bowling in the hallway.

236. Do yoga together.

237. Make a beanbag toss game.

238. Play checkers.

239. String popcorn.

240. Have a tea party.

241. Make homemade fingerpaint. (See Appendix C)

242.Paint a picture.

243. Pretend play pirates.

244. Stack plastic cups and try to knock them down.

245. Use a straw to transfer 20 marshmellows to a bowl in under one minute.

246. Build a town out of cardboard boxes.

247. Make Valentines cards for friends.

248. Pretend play bakery.

249. Play a game of chess.

250. Make a clean mud sensory bin. (See Appendix C)

251. Pretend play restaurant.

252. Play I Spy.

253. Make flubber. (See Appendix C)

254. Teach your child to sew or knit.

255. Work a puzzle together.

256. Make a stop motion movie.

257. Learn a magic trick.

258. Make paper snowflakes.

259. Pretend play astronauts.

260. Freeze toys in a muffin tin and throw the iced toys in the bath. The kids will enjoy watching them melt to revel the toy.

261. Break out the crayons and color together.

262. Peel the paper off broken crayons and melt them in a shaped trays.

263. Make sculpting foam. (See Appendix C)

264. Act out a favorite movie.

265. Make a lava lamp. Instructions online.

266. Make paper dolls.

267. Fill the sink with water and bubbles and let them play.

268. Pretend play detectives. Make clues for the kids to follow.

269. Play a matching game.

270. Bake brownies together.

271. Pretend play pet shop.

272. Have a drawing contest.

273. Have a pillow fight.

274. Make homemade playdough. (See Appendix C)

275. Make a road for toy cars with painter's tape.

276. Pretend play toy store.

277. Make sculptures with toothpicks and mini marshmallows.

278. Make paper mache. (See Appendix C)

279. Make a snowman pizza.

280. Toss glow sticks in the bath and turn out the lights.

281. Dress up and have a photo shoot.

282. Pretend play salon.

283. Play a dice game, like Yahtzee.

284. Make caramel apples.

285. Make cloud dough. (See Appendix C)

286. Paint kids' hands and place on a t-shirt. Write their name and age.

287. Make a marble run with paper towel tubes.

288. Find an easy science experiment online to try.

289. Write a comic strip with your child.

290. Read a joke book.

291. Fish for magnetic letters in the tub.

292. Paint each others faces with face paint.

293. Pretend play fire department.

294. Pull the couch cushions off and have kids jump from cushion to cushion and not touch the floor.

295. Make bread together.

296. Look through photo albums and baby books.

297. Play a card game.

298. Draw you family tree and talk about your heritage.

299. Tell stories of your childhood to your kids.

300. Set up a tent in your living room and camp out.

Places to Visit

301. Local craft fair.

302. Bowling alley.

303. Skating rink.

304. Aquarium.

305. Science museum.

306. Planetarium.

307. Art museum.

308. Local carnival.

309. Water park or local pool.

310. Bounce house.

311. Indoor play land.

312. Kid's restaurant with gaming.

313. Historical sites near you.

314. Local fair.

315. Library.

Holiday Play

Valentine's Day

316. Make salt dough valentines. Follow the same recipe for salt dough ornaments but cut them into hearts and add red food coloring. (See Appendix C)

317. Make Valentine's cards for your friends.

318. Leave love notes all over the house for your child. Have him go on a hunt to find them and collect them in a jar.

319. Read a Valentine's Day book.

320. Make heart-shaped treats.

321. Make a craft out of several different sizes of hearts.

323. Cut out colored hearts from construction paper and string them on yarn for a Valentine's Day garland.

324. Bake heart-shaped cookies.

Martin Luther King Jr. Day

325. Read a children's book about the civil rights movement.

326. Make a handprint peace dove craft.

327. Print a coloring page from the internet and color together.

St. Patrick's Day

328. Have green pancakes and green milk for breakfast (use a little green food coloring).

329. Make a leprechaun craft.

330. Make a shamrock craft.

331. Make shamrock slime. Use the slime recipe and add green food coloring. (See Appendix C)

Easter

332. Color eggs.

333. Hide the eggs and have the children find them.

334. Do a bunny craft.

335. Do a nativity craft.

336. Make salt dough eggs and paint them. (See Appendix C)

337. Make a mosaic cross craft.

338. Bake cookies and decorate with bunny faces or crosses.

Mother's Day

339. Write Mom a letter.

340. Make Mom a craft.

341. Make breakfast for Mom.

Memorial Day

342. Make a craft stick flag.

343. Make a patriotic pinwheel craft.

344. Bake a cake and decorate it like a flag.

Father's Day

345. Write Dad a letter.

346. Make Dad a craft.

347. Make lunch for Dad.

Independence Day

348. Go to a fireworks display.

349. Put sparklers in playdough cups to protect little hands.

350. Learn the lyrics to The Star Spangled Banner and sing.

351. Make fireworks by dropping paint on paper and blowing it with a straw in different directions.

Halloween

352. Dress up and go trick or treating.

353. Attend or host a Halloween party.

354. Make a ghost craft.

355. Make a pumpkin craft.

356. Watch The Great Pumpkin Charlie Brown

   Thanksgiving

357. Make a hand print turkey.

358. Make a thankful tree and write what you're thankful for on the leaves.

359. Make personalized place mats with hand prints and a laminator.

360. Make dinner together.

   Christmas

361. Make a Christmas countdown calendar.

362. Visit a live nativity.

363. Go see a holiday lights display.

364. Decorate the Christmas tree.

365. Make salt dough ornaments and use Christmas cookie cutter shapes. (See Appendix C)

Appendix C

Recipes for Homemade Fun

Salt Dough Ornaments: ½ cup salt, 1 cup flour, ½ cup water. Bake at 250 degrees for 2 hours or until thoroughly dried. Decorate with acrylic paints.

Cinnamon Dough Ornaments: 2 cups cinnamon, 1-1/2 cups applesauce. Mix cinnamon with 1 cup applesauce. Continue adding applesauce a little at a time until the dough reaches a firm consistency. Place dough on wax paper. Place a wood strip on each side far enough apart so the ends of your rolling pin can rest on them. Cover the dough with another piece of wax paper and roll to 1/4 " thick. Remove the top wax paper. Cut out shapes with cookie cutters. For hangers, use a straw to make a small hole at the top of each ornament. Transfer to a flat area where they can dry away from direct heat. Turn them often; it will take about 5 days for them to dry completely. After drying, use emery board to smooth the outer edges.

Cloud Dough: 8 cups of flour, 1 cup of baby oil or canola oil.

Homemade Play Dough: ½ cup salt, ½ cup water, 1

cup flour, food dye.

Homemade Bubbles: 3 cups of water, ½ cup light corn syrup, 1 cup dish soap (transparent/clear soap works best). Mix water and corn syrup until blended. Slowly stir in soap. This will last several weeks in an air-tight container.

Homemade Moon Sand: 6 cups play sand, 3 cups corn starch, 1-1/2 cups water, food coloring if desired.

Flour Paint: Flour, liquid paint, water. Combine equal parts of flour and paint. Add drops of water until it achieves desired consistency.

Sculpting Foam: 1 cup shaving cream (non-menthol), ½ cup of white glue, paint, glitter.

Oobleck: 1-1/2 cup cornstarch, 1 cup water, food coloring.

Sparkle Paint: 3 cups flour, 3 cups salt, 3 cups water, food coloring.

Flubber: 5 tbs of liquid starch, 2 cups of glue, 1-1/2 cups of water to mix with the glue, additional 1 cup of hot water to mix with the liquid starch, food coloring.

Mix 2 cups of glue and 1-1/2 cups of water in a big bowl. Add color if desired and stir. In the extra cup of hot water, dissolve 5 tbs of liquid starch. Stir well. After it is dissolved, pour the liquid starch mixture slowly into the glue and warm mixture. Mix with your hands or sturdy wooden spoon.

Paper-Mache: 2 cups cold water, 1-1/2 to 1-3/4 cups of flour, newspaper cut or torn into strips. Mix water and flour in a large bowl with a wire whisk until smooth. Mixture should be the consistency of heavy cream. Coat your mold (such as an inflated balloon) with one layer of the newspaper strips that have been dipped in water. Then dip strips into flour mixture and lay over the first layer until the mold is well coated. Allow to dry completely until your mold is hard. If desired, add another layer of newspaper strips that have been dipped in the flour mixture and allow to dry. Paint over the strips in any design or color of your choice.

Scratch and Sniff Watercolors: 1 tbs unsweetened powdered drink mix, 1 tbs warm water.

Crafty Clay (good for beads and small figurines): 1 cup cornstarch and baking soda in a small sauce pan. Add water and stir until mixture is smooth. Heat mixture for 5 minutes over medium heat. Stir until it begins to thicken and turn to dough. Remove from saucepan and allow it to cool. Knead dough 2-3 minutes. Let finished creation air-dry until hard.

Clay Dough: 1 cup of cornstarch, 2 cups of baking soda, 1-1/2 cups of water, food coloring of choice. Mix cornstarch, baking soda, water, and food coloring in a saucepan over the medium heat. Knead until it has a dough-like consistency.

Slime: 4 oz of Elmer's white glue, 1 1/2 cup of water, 1 tsp of Borax powder. Pour glue and 1/2 cup of water in a container. Add food coloring if desired. In a separate container, mix 1 cup of water with 1 tsp of Borax powder. Slowly stir glue mixutre into the Borax solution. Knead to proper consistency.

Giant Bubbles: 6 cups of water, 1/2 cup of blue Dawn dish liquid, 1/2 cup of corn flour, 1 tbs baking powder. To make the bubble wands, I threaded yarn through 2 straws and tied a knot to make a large square with the straws on 2 ends.

Sidewalk Chalk Paint: In a muffin tin, mix 1 part cornstarch to 1 part water. You can add more water for a thinner paint. Add food coloring.

Salt Clay: 1 cup flour, 3/4 cup salt, 1/2 cup water, 1/4 cup coooking oil, food coloring. Place flour, salt, and oil in a mixing bowl and stir. Combine water and food coloring, and gradually add the colored water to the flour mixture. When donw sculpting, bake to harden at 300 degrees for 1-2 hours.

Shaving Cream Paint: This is great for painting in the bath tub. Simply mix shaving cream (I use the kind for sensitive skin) with food coloring.

Clean Mud: 3 rolls of toilet paper, 1 bar of Ivory soap grated, 3/4 cup of Borax powder, water. Unroll the toilet paper into a large container. Saturate with water. Add ivory soap and Borax. Mix well.

Homemade Fingerpaint: 1/4 cup of liquid starch, 1 tbsp powdered tempera paint. Mix well until blended.

Appendix D

Resources for Positive Parents

Books:

1. Positive Parenting in Action by Rebecca Eanes and Laura Ling

2. Peaceful Parent, Happy Kids by Dr. Laura Markham

3. The Whole-Brain Child by Daniel Siegel and Tina Payne Bryson

4. No-Drama Discipline by Daniel Siegel and Tina Payne Bryson

5. Easy to Love, Difficult to Discipline by Becky Bailey

6. Two Thousand Kisses a Day by L.R.Knost

7. The Gentle Parent by L.R.Knost

8. Whispers Through Time by L.R.Knost

9. Jesus, the Gentle Parent by L.R.Knost

10. Hands Free Mama by Rachel Macy Stafford

11. Twelve Alternatives to Time Out by Ariadne Brill

12. If I Have to Tell You One More Time by Amy McCready

13. Siblings Without Rivalry by Faber and Mazlish

14. The Five Love Languages of Children by Gary Chapman and Ross Campbell

15. Hold On To Your Kids by Gordon Neufeld

16. Unconditional Parenting by Alfie Kohn

17. Playful Parenting by Lawrence Cohen

18. How to Talk So Kids Will Listen, and Listen So Kids Will Talk by Faber and Mazlish
19. Positive Discipline by Jane Nelsen
20. No Bad Kids: Toddler Discipline Without Shame by Janet Lansbury
21. Let the Baby Drive by Lu Hanessian
22. The Conscious Parent by Shefali Tsabary
23. Out of Control by Shefali Tsabary

Websites:
www.positive-parents.org
www.ahaparenting.com
www.janetlansbury.com
www.positiveparentingconnection.net
www.truparenting.net
www.parentingbeyondpunishment.com
www.handsfreemama.com
www.littleheartsbooks.com
www.stopspanking.org
www.teach-through-love.com
www.positiveparentingsolutions.com
www.elizabethpantley.com
www.parent2parentu.com
http://www.peacefulparent.com/
www.nospank.net
http://www.abundantmama.com/
www.brenebrown.com

www.goodjobandotherthings.com

http://dirtandboogers.com/

http://lemonlimeadventures.com/

www.creativewithkids.com

www.presenceparenting.com

www.authenticparenting.info

Websites for play ideas:

http://letslassothemoon.com/

www.handsonaswegrow.com

www.growingajeweledrose.com

http://www.playdoughtoplato.com/

****

For a more in-depth look at how to put positive parenting principles into practice, get _Positive Parenting in Action: The How-To Guide for Putting Positive Parenting Principles into Action in Early Childhood_, by Laura Ling and myself. In that book, we walk you through more than 40 scenarios including behaviors such as whining, aggression, lying, back talk, potty learning, sleep issues, and much more.

Visit my website at www.positive-parents.org

****

39087970R00104

Made in the USA
Lexington, KY
06 February 2015